Introduction

A genealogist must work from documentary evidence and ......, however trustworthy the source may seem, or however recently the event occurred. To compile a family tree, I tell my students, begin with yourself. The reason is simple; in 1998, in the process of researching my family history, I discovered an adoption which had remained a closely guarded family secret for forty-five years; my own.

As the shock and hurt began to recede, many things that had seemed inexplicable became clear. Encouraged by this, I set out to recover as much information as possible about my origins. I did not expect to be successful after so many years had elapsed, but over time I was able to assemble not just a family history, but knowledge of the particular events that led my mother giving me up for adoption. As part of the process, I met my birth brother for the first time.

This story is based on fact as nearly as possible under the circumstances. It has taken many years of searching, and investigation of those documents that could be located and are extant, before an account of the people and events could be assembled. Most of the people in this story I have never met, although I have used the facts I have been able to ascertain, and conversations with those members of the family still alive.

Gratitude and thanks are due to:
The Pepperpots
Carol Mathison
Kathy Wilshaw
Miranda Ponsonby, who supplied not just memories and information, but also photographs of my mother and her family.
Father Jeremy Davies and Terry Keeler for their help and kindness.
Pat Tudsbury of Cape Town for sharing memories of Hugh and Helen Tevis.
Glyn Gowans for his meticulous research which has been generously shared.
More recently my Ponsonby cousins, Siobhan Tulloch and Roger Gwynn, have provided material from the family archives and Trinity College, Dublin.
My sister Karin, niece Louise and brother Cary for memories and photographs.

I could not have envisaged this search for birth relatives without the love and encouragement of my husband and children, and the many friends and family who supported me through both good and bad times and stayed the course.

Last but by no means least, my brother Stefan, who believed in me.

Diane Weeks
2021

A Family Story

'Everyone tells stories, and all story tellers are liars. They have an excessive need to make sense of experience, and so things get twisted and shaped to suit. We fumble about in the fog, and patterns come to us eerily, like distant foghorns over water.' Erdal.

'The greatest hazard of all, losing one's self, can occur very quietly in the world, as if it were nothing at all.' Søren Kierkegaard

The 25th May 1997 was the day everything changed, forever; the catalyst a book languishing on a shelf for years, 'The History of our Family' emblazoned on its cover. I had never felt impelled to undertake the necessary research, until now. Today I intended to apply for a copy of my full birth certificate at the Family Records Office in Islington, something I had been putting off for years. Any mention to my parents of obtaining a full certificate met with such cold disapproval the issue had been evaded for longer than I cared to admit.

Examination of my short certificate did not suggest any irregularity. It was all in order; my full name, date and place of birth. It bore the official seal of the General Register Office and the date of extraction from the register. Why these doubts then? Perhaps it was the flicker of alarm across my mother's face when I asked what had happened to the original and her terse reply "It was lost when we moved house." It was clear she would not enter into further discussion. When I suggested building a family tree the response was equally dismissive "People who go digging about in the past seldom learn anything good about themselves", although she would not elaborate on this sweeping generalisation. Was I about to open a Pandora's Box of unpalatable secrets? Despite earlier misgivings, on that fateful morning I felt buoyed up by anticipation. Finally, I would lay the matter to rest once and for all.

At first glance the archives at The Family Records Centre in Islington were intimidating. The hushed intensity of researchers' intent on their task emphasised my lack of experience. I was grateful for my husbands' company. "Shall we ask...?" I queried,

"No need. Look, the rows are labelled, we need Births, second quarter 1952". It was surprisingly simple to find the necessary ledger, flip through the pages to surnames beginning with K. Dave peered over my shoulder as I ran a finger down the list, once, twice; nothing, Diane Lynn Kett was missing. Surely there had to be a mistake? Now that my suspicions were about to be proved correct, I did not want to accept the evidence. Dave whistled softly under his breath; turning to look at him I saw the certainty in his eyes, "You were adopted" he said. In a daze I allowed myself to be propelled to the back of the archives, where it was quieter, less frequented. These shelves held the adoption records. In the volume 'Adoptions 1949 – 1960'; my name, 'Diane Lynn Kett' alongside a date, 27th March 1953.

In the café Dave handed me a lukewarm coffee. Behind his forced smile I could see the shock in his face. My head was awash with conflicting emotions; hurt, anger, disbelief, sadness, and something that felt strangely akin to euphoria. I experienced a moment of pure relief, of freedom, of being unchained from invisible shackles.

After completing the forms to obtain a full birth certificate I learned that this would not be sent in the post, but handed to me in person by a Social Worker. Infuriatingly there would be a long wait, but I was somewhat consoled by the idea that this forced delay would provide time to begin adjusting to a new reality.

Yet an odd thing, I discovered, during that strangest of times, was an ability to continue day to day interaction with my parents (my adoptive parents!) without any discernible difference. Could I ever admit to having uncovered their secret? I was about to learn the time for this had passed. Later that week mum and I attended hospital for some test results which had seemed innocuous beforehand. But when the consultant glanced over from the couch where he was examining my mother and I caught an almost imperceptible shake of his head, my stomach dipped with fear. Mum did not have long. If I ever intended to broach the subject with my parents, that option was now put firmly from my mind.

A year passed before I was invited to meet a Social Worker at Essex Social Services. Many times, during that year, I rehearsed this meeting in my imagination, summoning up what seemed to me a likely scenario; my birth mother a relative or friend of the family, perhaps a young unmarried girl, given no choice but to leave her baby with nuns or an orphanage? The uncertainty would soon be over. I entered the office buildings, pressed the button for the lift and arrived at first floor reception, where I was asked to wait. The delay was mercifully brief before I was sitting opposite a young woman, Emma, a brown folder on the table between us. Her approach was business-like, "Can I ask how much you know of your adoption, and what sort of information you are expecting?"

How ridiculous to have to tell this stranger that I know absolutely nothing. My head pounding, I summoned every ounce of will to maintain a similarly detached facade, "I don't know anything at all. My parents never spoke of it. My mother died last year, and my father is in poor health." Emma remained impassive as she selected a document from the file. "This is your original birth certificate. Are any of the names familiar?" They were not. My given name was Marie Louise Nada, my mother's name, Andree Nada, 'usual residence' an address in Knightsbridge. Unsurprisingly the space for father's name had a line scored through.

"You'll need to do some research if you want to find out more." Emma neatly side stepped any assumption I might have held that she could assist.

There were many more sheets of paper in the file, and Emma methodically dealt with each, accentuating the most important pieces of information. "Your mother was married to a Swedish national, who divorced her for adultery. When your mother signed the adoption papers, she was a patient at a private hospital in York, suffering trauma and ill health as a result of divorce and the birth of her child."

Although my mother's name was entered on my birth certificate as Andree Nada (formerly Davies), court papers and various letters addressed her as Mrs. Sandgren. At any rate it was clear that Nada was not a surname, but a given name.

"There is another child mentioned here, you have a brother or sister." Emma paused to see the effect this was having, and I hoped I gave the impression of calmly assimilating the news. In reality, I had retreated to a place where each disclosure could be viewed dispassionately, remotely, as though about someone else. I could not make a connection between myself and the name on the birth certificate – Marie Louise Nada – it was not possible to accept they were one and the same person. I dragged my attention back to Emma, "……. your mother requested a photograph of you to be sent, before she signed the adoption papers".

Such a pitifully small request, handwritten, 'Mrs. Sandgren has requested a photograph of the infant; she is emphatic that she will not require another at a later date or wish to see the child.' It was the only human touch in an otherwise official clutch of papers and correspondence between my birth mother's solicitors and the children's department at West Ham. Emma explained that until the 1960s an adopted child was given a new identity, and the birth parents or parent would find it impossible to trace their child, or find out how they fared after the adoption was finalised.

"Would you like details of an organisation which can help, should you decide to trace your birth family?" I noted down the organisation's name and address before asking, "All this information is very old. Is there anything more up to date to go on? Did my mother ever make contact again?"

"Nothing, I'm afraid. This has all been stored here for the past forty-five years. Now it's over to you, I wish you luck."

I left with my head reeling, feeling flimsy and insubstantial; I could be anyone now, which in reality meant I was no one.

Half remembered images and conversations floated in my head; "Ignorance is bliss. What the eyes don't see the heart won't grieve over," mum had quoted. Dad would frequently assert that I had mum's eyes, but I saw no resemblance to her now when I looked in the mirror.

Nevertheless, I found it easier to accept the fact of my adoption whilst I did not share it. Apart from Dave, no one knew. What I mean is that I told no one what I knew. Every single member of my family, every friend above a certain age, must have known and willingly or perhaps unwillingly, colluded in the lie.

Even my children remained in ignorance. While it remained a secret, there was a part of me which did not have to acknowledge the reality; Emma's words echoed 'You'll know you've reached acceptance when you can drop your adoption casually into the conversation, like your address, or occupation, it's a part of your life, but it isn't *who* you are.'

It was actually surprisingly easy, once I made up my mind. I had to start somewhere and chose my daughter and son.

Sarah didn't take it well, 'I'm no more related to my cousins than the person I sit next to on the bus', she bemoaned. Ian, younger and by nature more pragmatic, merely commented 'Well, you're still my mum, whatever anyone else is,' and no one could argue with that.

On a wave of disclosure, I called my brother Martin, who I knew was mum and dad's natural son, having checked his birth details at the Record Office. This was a difficult call, as I needed to arrange to see him alone, which wasn't usual. Unwittingly I was the cause of a sleepless night as my brother and sister-in-law considered all the dread possibilities which might have resulted in my request to see Martin alone as soon as possible. My confession, which I had expected to cause some degree of shock and distress, was met only with relief. Martin called his wife to give her the news, "It's OK," I heard him say, "it's only that Di just found out she was adopted."

Feeling a certain weight had lifted I joined NORCAP, the organisation dedicated to searching for birth relatives, and purchased books to help the cause. I knew from the court papers Emma had supplied that my mother's name was Andree Nada Sandgren (known as Nada), formerly Davies, and that in 1952 her address was 29 Montpelier Place, Knightsbridge.

The building on the left with the clock outside is 396 Commercial Road, the East End Maternity Hospital where I was born, the houses on the right are Montpelier Place, Knightsbridge, where Nada was living. What circumstances had led to someone from such an affluent background being obliged to give birth on the opposite side of town? Nada's doctor's address on the adoption paper was in Harley Street, so why was I born at a hospital in the East End?

Dave was adamant that I should not waste time on such ponderings, as most of my questions would surely be answered with further research. To this end we began to plan methodically, the next step being a return to the Family Record Centre to locate my mother's birth record. To my great dismay there was no entry for Andree Nada under the surname Davies. I was discouraged that it may not have been her real name, but a cypher, the dictionary definition of Nada being *'Nothing, thing born, small, insignificant thing'*. Returning home via the Westminster archives, however, I was overjoyed to discover an electoral roll which confirmed that living at 29 Montpelier Place in 1948 was head of household Elizabeth Prudence Davies and another resident, Nada Davies.

"It still doesn't explain why we can't find any record of your mother's birth" Dave pointed out, and at that juncture we felt as though we had hit the proverbial brick wall.

Just as it seemed we would be thwarted at the first hurdle I received a surprising phone call from my intermediary at NORCAP, Carol, "There's a good reason you can't find an entry for your mother's birth. Her mother Elizabeth married twice. The second husband was a man called Idris

Meredyth Davies. They married in 1931, and Idris adopted Nada later the same year, changing her surname from Tevis to Davies."

A further visit to the Family Records and I was finally in possession of Nada's birth certificate containing two vital new pieces of information, the most important of which was my grandfather's name – Hugh Tevis **(see Appendix 5),** and the address where Nada was born – Cransford Hall, Suffolk. I was greatly encouraged by this, feeling certain it would be a relatively simple matter to track the family down: Tevis is an unusual surname. Hugh's occupation, 'Gentleman', a puzzle. I had no idea that being a gentleman counted as an occupation. It made my grandfather seem rather grand, and impossibly remote.

I wrote to the Suffolk Family History Society enquiring about the inhabitants of Cransford Hall during the 1950s and received a prompt, but ultimately disappointing reply, to the effect that as far as anyone knew the house had always been owned by Sir Patrick Hamilton. The Tevis's must either have rented the house for a time, or were guests of the Hamilton's when Nada was born. However, this did not deter me from a visit to the Suffolk records office in Ipswich to check the 1950's electoral rolls. This confirmed the information provided by the Suffolk Family History Society, there was no mention of the Tevis name. If my family had ever lived there, this was not in evidence.

The Hall, Cransford

Nevertheless, we decided to drive over to the Hall to see for ourselves. Wrought iron gates at the entrance to the drive stood open, leaving us free to proceed towards a shielding glade, which once passed revealed a magnificent Elizabethan manor house. As we approached, evidence of renovation work became apparent. Much of the façade was covered with scaffolding and a builder's van was parked by the entrance. A notice announced the building was in the process of being converted to a nursing home. Returning the same way, I spied an elderly woman in the garden of the gate keeper's cottage. Dave pulled over but the woman seemed suspicious of my questioning, answering only with a shake of her head. It was dispiriting to realise I had to return home without a shred of new information.

While my NORCAP contact, Carol, submitted enquiries on my behalf to various agencies which only communicate via official representatives, I continued to make headway at the Family Records Centre. My mother's birth certificate provided her mother's name, Elizabeth Prudence Tevis, formerly Ponsonby, another unusual name, making it relatively simple to locate her in the indexes.

When the certificate arrived, I was intrigued to see that Elizabeth's father was William Ponsonby **(see Appendix 1),** a Captain with the 3rd Dragoon Guards. At Southend library an edition of the national biography 'Who Was Who', revealed a photograph of William, looking handsome and self-possessed in army uniform. The entry provided brief details of his life; 'born August 1874 the eldest surviving son of Colonel Justinian Gordon Ponsonby. He served in the South African War in Thorneycroft's Mounted Infantry, and was created a Companion of the Distinguished Service Order in 1901, in recognition of services during the operations in South Africa, presented by the

King 29 October 1901. In 1902 he married Lilian Patteson Nickalls daughter of Sir Patteson Nickalls and Florence Womersley. He died 18th January 1919.'

Curious to find out more, I located a military historian who offered to undertake research at the National Archives at Kew on my behalf. I received a speedy reply, "There is rather a large file available on William Ponsonby – but you may be somewhat perturbed by the contents. It would appear that William lost his commission due to disorderly conduct, among other things. If you would still like me to obtain it for you, I shall do so tomorrow."

The ease with which I was able to extract details from long ago was in stark contrast to my current investigations; The Law Society to whom I had written requesting details of the solicitors involved with my adoption informed me one of the partners had died nearly thirty years previously, the other, John Dyson, whose signature graced so many of the documents, died only recently; they regretted all documents referring to my mother had been destroyed.

A solicitor in Sweden I commissioned to investigate the whereabouts of the man Nada married in 1951 had found only one person living in Sweden today with this name, and after some enquiries had concluded he was not the same person. I filed the letter away with a heavy heart, realising there were few avenues left to explore. Almost every line of enquiry had been exhausted. One however, did remain, and this was The Retreat in York where Nada had been a patient. A Notary Public had visited her there in 1953, to obtain a signature on my adoption papers. A search of the internet showed the institution still existed, specialising in mental health problems including drug and alcohol abuse. I was amazed to read that all ex-patients' files were stored in their archives but was politely informed that although the information on my mother would still be held, this did not necessarily mean it could be disclosed. I wrote directly to the chief executive, only to receive a firm, but kind refusal to divulge any information on the grounds of patient confidentiality.

A rather odd sounding enquiry, known as 'dead or not dead' entailed writing to the NHS central register to enquire the name and address of a person's GP. The reply was brief and to the point: 'From the information supplied by your letter I was able to identify your birth mother. It is with the deepest regret I have to inform you that your mother died on 27th January 1971 in Lewisham. I cannot assist you any further with this matter.'

I should have been neither shocked nor surprised, but in fact I was floored. Nada had died when she was just 44 years old, and I was 19, long before I discovered the truth about my past, so there had never been any possibility of a meeting between us. Nevertheless, it would be possible to see where and how my mother had died, by applying for her death certificate. Easier said than done, as there was nothing to indicate Nada's surname at the time, which would mean ploughing through every entry in the register, looking for an Andree Nada. Dave suggested a new tactic – I should begin searching at A and he would begin at Z. This turned out to be inspirational as within minutes Dave had located a death under the surname Yardley. When Nada's death certificate arrived, I learned my mother had died at Lewisham Hospital on the 27th January 1971, and her residence at the time was also in Lewisham. The nearest cemetery,

Hither Green, responded swiftly to my enquiry with a letter confirming Nada's date of burial and a map showing the number and area of her grave. When I visited the cemetery the following Sunday, expecting a graveyard with rows of headstones marking each plot, I discovered the area containing public graves was more like a meadow, with few memorials. The grave number was of little use, as there were too few markers to work out where Nada would have been laid to rest. It was a gusty day, the sky full of birdsong and for the first time, I placed a spray of white lilies on the ground and thought of the woman who had given me life and whom I would never know.

Long after, when I had found and met my brother, we arranged to have a memorial made and placed at the head of Nada's grave. The inscription reads 'In/Loving Memory of/Our Dear Mother/ANDREE NADA/8.9.1926 – 27.1.1971/Who was lost/And is found/Stefan and Diane (Marie-Louise)/Goodbye Ruby Tuesday

*

The imperative of having a disinterested intermediary beavering away on my behalf became apparent when Carol from NORCAP phoned on a bleak winter day late in the year 2000, just as I was beginning to think there would be no breakthrough. It was immediately obvious she had some interesting news to impart,

"I found a member of NORCAP resident in Sweden. His name's Guy" Carol explained. "I contacted him some time ago, asking if he would be prepared to undertake research on your behalf, and he's agreed. His surname is Davies, too, so this should help matters along. Sweden is an open country in any case. There are few restrictions on obtaining information – he will find out where your mother married, and if your sibling was born in Sweden."

The optimism this news brought was short lived, as a reply was e-mailed from Guy almost at once.

'Your mother's husband died in 1980 – sorry to have to give you such disappointing news. I will continue to look for their marriage entry at each parish. There are no centralised records. I'll let you know as soon as I have news.'

A further email arrived in February 2001:

'I have located your mother's marriage entry in the wedding book at Englebrecht. Nada Davies married Stig Sandgren on the 22nd March, 1951. I also have the following – Nada gave birth to a boy – called Stefan – on the 28th March, 1951. Stig divorced Nada for adultery in February 1953. I have the number of the case, and can apply for the papers.'

At last, I was in possession of concrete facts – the date and place of my mother's marriage, my brother's name and date of birth.

A few weeks later Guy telephoned with the news that the divorce file had arrived. It was quite bulky, yet already Guy had translated the essence, and was keen to impart it.

'Your father is mentioned, he's the co-respondent in the divorce. It gives his name and an address; I've had a look in the phone book – there's only one person of this name in Stockholm – it must be him.' I noted the name and address having already made the decision to write. Guy hesitated, 'There's something else. I've made further enquiries. You'll need to handle this very carefully; great sensitivity will be needed. You see your father was already married, and his wife pregnant with their first child when you were conceived. His wife died some years ago, but his four children are all still living in Sweden'.

His message safely delivered, Guy must have been relieved to put down the receiver but not before he had given me the name and phone number of a Swedish organisation helping to reunite adopted adults with their birth families. My call was answered immediately by a lady called Annelie, who spoke perfect English and was quite unperturbed by my story. Having handled many birth family reunions, Annelie sounded full of confidence 'Don't worry, you can write to your father and I will translate the letter, and send it on. He can first make contact with me. We will not involve you at first. We can see what his reaction is, before you speak to him.' I was relieved not to have to drop the initial bombshell myself. What do you say to a parent you have never met 'Hello, I'm your daughter, shall we meet?' On the other hand, I did not want to sound apologetic, so kept to the point in a brief request, and imagined my letter passing through many hands, translated and in a new envelope, sliding through my father's letter box and landing innocuously on the mat, along with the bills and junk mail.

The lean years of the occasional crumb of information coming my way were suddenly replaced by information arriving thick and fast. My first task on arriving home in the evening was to switch on the computer and scan the emails for a message from one of my contacts.
Guy was the first to impart more news:
'There's something new I've gleaned from the divorce file - your grandmother Elizabeth was killed in an accident shortly before your birth. She died in a plane crash at Frankfurt, en route from South Africa, where she had been spending the winter with Hugh.'
I had not considered the possibility of Elizabeth and Hugh remaining on good terms despite separating and then divorcing soon after Nada's birth. Typing 'Hugh Tevis' into the search engine caused the screen to blank for a few seconds before three items appeared mentioning his name. All were in South Africa.
Carol was able to provide the name of a social worker in Johannesburg, but the reply was not encouraging.
'Thanks for your letter which I received a few days ago. I tried looking for Hugh Tevis on a copy of the voters roll for 1979, but he is not mentioned. Nor were there any other Tevis' listed.
Tracing in South Africa is much more difficult than the UK as the public is denied access to birth, marriage and death registers. I think the best person to approach with regard to your search for your grandfather would be a genealogist.
The only other thing I could try is to ask a certain radio programme to broadcast a message asking the listeners if they know of his whereabouts.
Kind regards
 Kay.'
I took up the suggestion right away and spent some time composing a message for the radio programme that was brief yet included all the pertinent points.
I also contacted a genealogist in South Africa, and sent photocopies of all relevant documents to a lady called Valda Napier who was highly recommended.
While awaiting a possible response from my father in Sweden, and the radio broadcast, I visited the city library where past copies of The Times newspaper are available on microfiche, and began searching for a report of the plane crash in which my grandmother perished. If the plan had been for her to return home before Nada gave birth, this would probably have been during March. It seemed likely that an airline disaster would make the front page, but I couldn't be sure, so doggedly scanned each paper front to back, from the 1st March 1952. It wasn't until my fourth visit to the library that the headline for Monday March 24th made my heart leap into my throat, 'Frankfurt airliner disaster, 44 now dead. The airliner - a Douglas Globemaster on the KLM service Johannesburg-Rome-Amsterdam – was to have made an intermediate landing at the Rhein-Main airport......... According to eye witnesses and one of the survivors, the aircraft came out of a patch of mist above a forest. She was then so low that the tops of trees were torn off, and she lost two of her engines and a wing, and crashed after having cut a long swathe through the forest. Parts of the aircraft were thrown over a wide area. An explosion occurred, and fire broke out. The passengers, who had already fastened their seatbelts preparatory to landing, were flung together in the fore part of the aircraft. A forester and other helpers brought out six persons, before fire drove them away, but two were already dead, and a third died later. One of

the two women rescued was returning with her husband from honeymoon in Rome. He was among the killed.......'

Praying my grandmother had died before the flames reached her, I printed a copy of the article and the death announcement:

'Davies – On March 22, 1952, at Frankfurt, as the result of an air accident, Elizabeth Prudence (Prue) Davies, of 29 Montpelier Place, London. Dearly loved mother of Nada, Rhodri and Jeremy.'

There was a great deal to contemplate that evening, and an email from Kay in South Africa added to the mix; 'I am happy to tell you that, much to my surprise, a gentleman called into the radio station about the broadcast. He said Hugh died about ten years ago, and was a very colourful character. The respondent gave the name of someone in Australia who knows a lot about Hugh. I have passed all the information on to Valda, so I expect you will be contacting her in due course.'

How tantalising was this little titbit of information that might prove so promising. It told me so much and so little. Who was the mystery person in Australia? What exactly was meant by a 'colourful character' a term which might imply someone a little eccentric, or who lives outside societal norms?

Annelie phoned from Sweden the following day; her kindness could not disguise the ultimate tone of my father's response. He had been 'shocked', and 'disturbed'. He was not angry, she said, but he had not welcomed the news either. Try as I might to convince myself that I had not been expecting any kind of welcome, I had anticipated curiosity at least.

Annelie advised patience. She thought that after so long it might well take Gosta some time to come around to accepting that I had found him. Once he had assimilated this, he might agree to a meeting, or at least an exchange of photographs. 'Wait and see' was Annelies' final comment.

After so much anticipation there were more disappointments in the pipeline. Valda e-mailed from Johannesburg: 'I am still awaiting a reply from the gentleman in Australia. I have faxed him all your papers, as he wished to confirm the details before he responded. I am hoping to hear from him over the week-end. I have a feeling we will learn a lot more about your biological family than anticipated. With time I am certain we can obtain all the facts.'

I did not hear over the week-end, or during the following week. The extended wait for news began to play on my nerves leaving me jaded and edgy. Every day the list of emails was eagerly scanned, every day there was only disappointment.

When a message finally arrived, I could scarcely absorb the contents, the words refusing to connect;

'I have been busy the past week or so communicating with the gentleman in Australia by phone and fax. Following these enquiries, I have now located your brother, Stefan, and have been informed he will be phoning me. Apparently, he has also been trying to locate his family for many years, to no avail....'

The only piece of information I assimilated was that Stefan, my brother, had been located. But what exactly did Valda mean by 'located'? From initial euphoria, doubts crept in – why hadn't I heard directly from him? Why didn't Valda provide me with his address or phone number? The lack of detailed information was enervating and I quickly fell prey to doubts and uncertainties. I could not reply, was too afraid the mood had changed subtly, that everything would tail off for no apparent reason. While I was still staring at the screen indecisively, an incoming message flagged up with the subject line 'Wonderful News from Valda' and I knew immediately my worst fears were unfounded. Here was Stefan's address in the USA, his home and work phone numbers and e-mail, and a request to contact him as soon as possible. Valda also forwarded an email from Stefan headed "Saving the best 'til last".

After I sent a message arranging to telephone Stefan Saturday afternoon, the rest of the working week was intolerable. I simply wished it to be Saturday.

The wait was not quite that long however; on Friday evening Dave surprised me by opening the front door before I reached the step; it was clear he had important news to impart. Stefan had telephoned. It seemed a good thing that Dave had been first to speak to him. Somehow it diffused much of the tension and made it easier to return the call. My anxiety drained away and once the initial awkward exchanges were behind us, I found conversation surprisingly easy. The wariness and reserve I had expected were completely absent.

Stefan spoke openly of being abandoned at an Edinburgh orphanage at the age of just six months, his welfare overseen by Nada's godmother, Lady Playfair. There were infrequent visits from our mother, and he had no clear recollections of her.

Shortly before his fourth birthday, in what must have seemed like an event from a fairy story, a tall, handsome man arrived in a chauffeur driven Bentley, removed Stefan from the orphanage and onto his private yacht sailing to Africa. This was our grandfather Hugh Tevis, who acted 'in loco parentis' and changed Stefan's surname to his own. Stefan called Hugh 'Papa', and assumed he was his father until Hugh divulged the true nature of the relationship when Stefan was thirteen years old.

Before coming to collect him, Hugh had sent Stefan a photo, with a note on the back.

IN THIS PICURE THEY ARE
BANANAS. THE FARM IS IN A
LOVELY PART OF THIS COUNTRY. I
GROW TABACCO AND RAISE CATTLE.
SOME DAY SOON I HOPE YOU WILL
SEE IT TOO. LOVE PAPA.

On the subject of Nada, Hugh maintained a steely silence, his only words being that she was 'not a suitable person to know'.

After Hugh's death Stefan traced everyone who had known Nada, but they either would not, or could not, divulge any information. The genealogist whose help Stefan enlisted found few traces, and eventually the conclusion was reached that he had no living family, and would never find anything further.

During Stefan's childhood, Hugh had spent much of the time overseas, dealing with his many business interests and it was a case of 'out of sight is out of mind' for those he left behind. Despite Hugh's emotional detachment the years Stefan spent at the farm in Rhodesia provided a sense of belonging, until the idyll was shattered by being sent to Boarding School at the age of seven. During the holidays Hugh would usually foist Stefan off onto friends or distant relatives. Stefan explained 'I had plenty of offers of hospitality and lots of friends, but Hugh was my only family and I wanted to be with him. I was often lonely. Some of Hugh's friends were good to me, others less so. They had parties, drank too much. Sometimes I'd come across them – well, I wasn't meant to, you understand, that's why he tried to find other places for me to spend the holidays......'His voice trailed off, but he quickly collected himself, 'Perhaps I should tell you more about our family history'. I agreed; eager to distract him from more disturbing memories.

*

The slow deterioration in the family fortunes began with Hugh. His wife, Elizabeth Prudence Ponsonby (known as Prue) **(Appendix 10)**, an heiress in her own right, was not dependent on Hugh's wealth; they agreed a divorce settlement of around £1500 a year for Nada's upbringing. Perhaps Prue was discountenanced on discovering the true nature of Hugh's sexuality, and this may have been the root cause of her disaffection for Nada. At any rate, Nada was left no money or real estate in her mother's will, her share meriting only one line – 'my diamond pin'. Elizabeth took Nada to live in New York a few years after her divorce from Hugh, and there met the man who was to become her second husband, Idris Meredith Davies.

11

By this time Hugh was settled largely in Africa, where he owned a tobacco and maize farm in Rhodesia and various mining and business interests in the Cape, where he lived at a house called Monterey, in Bishopscourt. His fortunes did not flourish, there are rumours of blackmail at a time when homosexuality was not tolerated, and any hint of scandal would have been the kiss of death. Monterey was sold in 1952, and the farm in 1963. By the time Stefan completed his schooling at Millfield in Somerset, the fees were paid for by Hugh's third wife, Barbara Jean, who willingly accepted the burden of family finances.

Stefan told me 'Hugh needed the appearance of conventionality. Barbara did care for him and support him when his money ran out, although they argued all the time. Barbara drank heavily, too. After she died, I found bottles hidden all over the house. I've always been very grateful to Hugh for bringing me up. He didn't have to take responsibility.'

I was not too sure of that; in my world grandparents take responsibility for their grandchildren under far more challenging circumstances, yet it seemed that my privileged birth family held no such scruples.

Stefan and his wife Carla invited us to stay at their home in Salt Lake City that summer. However, as Dave had pressing work commitments, only I was free to travel. Several friends thought this trip into the unknown foolhardy and fraught with potential pitfalls, but I had my family's support which was what really mattered. I booked a flight for the earliest week-end I could arrange to leave, and began preparations. In the days before departure, I was touched by visits from the same friends who had initially urged caution, bringing cards and gifts - a diary to record my experiences, a brooch to wear, a good-luck charm - so that I went armed with talismans, like a pilgrim.

Dave's unequivocal support of the venture lasted until we reached the airport. Our daughter Sarah accompanied us and we whiled away the last minutes by ordering coffee and pastries. Sarah had no qualms about my trip, but Dave suddenly revised his earlier conviction that it was the right thing to do.

'Really Dad', Sarah sighed, 'you should have said something sooner, it's too late now.'

I was also suffering last minute nerves; the realisation that once I stepped onto the plane there was no turning back, and I appreciated Sarah's concise observation. Besides, I have learned to trust my inner voice, which was urging me to throw caution to the wind and go.

Seated in the aircraft, anxiety melted away. Five thousand miles away, Salt Lake City waited nestled in a valley high in the Rockies, a place of dreams. My own dream, about to be realised, was of the perfect American family – shiny, happy people.

A novel I had long intended to read kept me engrossed on the first leg of the journey. A short stopover in Boston provided only the briefest opportunity to refresh, before boarding again for the connecting flight among garrulous Midwesterners. The couple sitting next to me entered into conversation almost as soon as we were seated, and I was grateful for the diversion as the moment of my first meeting with Stefan and his family drew closer.

City lights sparkled below as the plane began the descent, the distant mountains a deeper black against the night sky. After travelling for almost seventeen hours, I should have been exhausted, but was instead elated and filled with anticipation, although no one seemed to be waiting for me among the friends and relatives greeting one another in the terminal building. Following signs to baggage reclaim, and hoping to find Stefan and his family there, I caught sight of someone striding briskly in my direction on the opposite side of the moving walkway, leaning across the barrier as he neared. We made the connection at the same moment and I leapt from the travellator just as Carla arrived laden with bags and baby Christian in his stroller. It seemed natural to hug like old friends, everyone speaking at once; excited, inarticulate greetings. Carla occupied herself with the camera, while my baby nephew, looking momentarily as though he might cry, changed his mind and joined in the celebrations.

After collecting my luggage, we climbed aboard their SUV, and a moment later were speeding along the interstate toward the city. Everywhere lights twinkled in the clear air, and I could see the mountains more clearly now, deeply shadowed against the velvet sky. Christian sat alongside in his baby seat, staring with frank curiosity while Carla entertained us with anecdotes of a wedding they had attended earlier in the day, leaving me free to remain silent while surreptitiously studying my new found family. By the time we arrived I felt utterly drained. Stefan and Carla directed me to the freshly decorated bedroom they had prepared for my visit. A bowl of flowers scented the air, and everything I could possibly need had been provided. Family photos were displayed in a frame on the cabinet as Stefan was eager to ensure I felt at home, 'Our home is yours too now,' were his final words as we said goodnight and I collapsed into bed.

Despite overwhelming exhaustion, I slept only fitfully, woke early, and made a phone call home. Dave was working in the garden, sounding tired and tense, and we had an unsatisfactory conversation before I hung up, exasperated. I felt unable to communicate my feelings, and Dave had been in an unresponsive mood.

Overhead I could hear the staccato pattering of Christian's footsteps, a sure signal the day had officially begun. We settled comfortably together to share breakfast, and I was struck by the intensely absorbed relationship between Stefan and his baby son. Carla smiled proudly across the table at the two of them, Christian bouncing in bare feet, one arm round his father's neck, 'Christian slept in our bed for a whole year! Can you believe that? – so that his face was the first thing Stef saw when he woke each morning.'

Carla's large exuberant family gathered round to assure me I was now included in their number. Everyone wanted to share in Stefan's good fortune at finding family he hadn't known existed, and I became a minor celebrity, receiving so many invitations over the week that it was difficult to find time for them all. The story of our reunion was told over and over, while Stefan nervously paced up and down, interrupting now and again to interject some remark. There was little time for us to talk in private, although Carla did arrange a lunch just for the two of us. I asked her if she was sorry to discover an 'in-law', if after all she hadn't preferred having Stefan to herself. 'Oh, I'm glad not to have a mother-in-law,' she replied with a laugh, 'but I guess I always wanted an older sister, and now I have one.'

There were many subjects I hoped to discuss with Stefan, but opportunity never presented itself. This was exacerbated by his working long hours most days, as publishing deadlines were approaching. Despite so many distractions, I was well aware that the outward persona Stefan wore – the devoted husband and father, the successful businessman, was a smokescreen for a much more complicated picture. He possessed a quality of perpetual restlessness, sometimes seeming as though in mind and spirit, he was elsewhere.

It seemed I was no closer to knowing him at all, that I was simply projecting the person I wanted him to be and finding that image reflected back.

On the final evening of my stay Stefan and Carla held a farewell party and long after the last guest departed, we sat late in the warmth of the garden, stars fluorescing overhead. I was painfully aware of the imminence of departure and the many questions I feared to ask, or have answered. Now I was alone with my new found brother and sister-in-law on my last evening I floundered, no longer feeling secure. It was all too new, too insubstantial. Carla, echoing my own need for a commitment to our mutual future, said, 'If Stefan is granted citizenship by the autumn, we could come to England after Christmas.'

Stefan whilst concurring that this was a good idea, appeared preoccupied and distracted. The efforts of the day seemed to have exhausted him, he looked drained, but more than that, somehow diminished. I felt again the undercurrent of something not quite right but was too unsure of my position for close enquiry. Little Christian, no doubt unsettled by the party, appeared on the decking clutching his pillow and trailing a small blue blanket. He made his way unhesitatingly, as always, straight to his dad. But then he did an odd thing. Instead of wanting to be cuddled and soothed back to sleep, he climbed onto the sofa and arranged the pillow behind his dad's head, tucking the blanket carefully under his chin, almost protectively, as though sensing how weary he was. Satisfied he had secured Stefan's comfort he curled up and closed his eyes. Something about the little boy's loving tenderness towards his father felt unbearably poignant. Perhaps it was the knowledge that Stefan had lived all his boyhood in the absence of such small tokens of family love.

Excusing myself on the need to rest before the long journey, I kissed each of them goodnight and made my way to bed.

The drive back to the airport along the same route we had taken on my arrival just a week ago seemed to belong to a previous life. The Rolling Stones 'Ruby Tuesday' played on the car stereo:

> 'Goodbye Ruby Tuesday
> Who can hang a name on you?
> When you change with every new day
> Still I'm going to miss you.'

"This song always makes me think of our mother" Stefan said. I was touched by his use of 'our' rather than the possessive 'my' mother and the uncertainties of the previous evening lifted. I began to feel more optimism for the future, until his next remark, only half-joking, "I'm afraid you won't like me when you know me better, I've lived most of my life as a moody, selfish, arrogant son-of-a-bitch."

My return home was joyful and emotional. We had missed one another and lunched out together on Sunday with a mutual appreciation that had not been so visible of late. By separating and reforming, the currency of our day to day lives had been revalued. Life suddenly felt full of possibilities, doors opening where previously no door had been visible.

I was disconcerted over the coming weeks, however, by the sporadic nature of contact with Stefan. Promised phone calls did not materialise and on one occasion when I reached Stefan at work, he was agitated and abruptly hung up. At the weekend his low lacklustre voice offered unconvincing apologies and my hunch that all was not well hardened into conviction. Even Carla was evasive, our conversations always curtailed by some interruption or other, and long after I replaced the receiver the air felt weighted with the burden of words unsaid.

*

At the beginning of October, I wrote again to The Retreat, the hospital founded by Quakers, where our mother Nada had been a patient. This time I enclosed a copy of Nada's death certificate in the hope they would agree to release some information to me as next of kin. The reply was something of a surprise. 'I would be happy to arrange to have your birthmother's notes photocopied. You may like to visit us and view them here. It may be that you would find this both interesting and helpful.......'

An information booklet accompanied the letter, and I learned that the hospital is now famous throughout the world for its pioneering approach to mental illness 'The Retreat occupies a central place in the history of psychiatry. Every textbook on the subject mentions the unique part played by our organisation in the reshaping of attitudes to towards people who are mentally ill.

Opened in 1796 by William Tuke, a retired tea merchant, the original Retreat was intended to be a place where members of The Society of Friends (Quakers) who were experiencing mental distress could recover in an environment that would be both familiar and sympathetic to their needs. Some years earlier, a Leeds Quaker, Hannah Mills, had died in the squalid and inhumane conditions that then prevailed in the York Asylum, and appalled at this, Tuke and his family vowed that never again should any Quaker be forced to endure such treatment.

The Retreat was based on the Quaker belief that there is 'that of God' in every person, regardless of any mental or emotional disturbance. Although to many modern-day mental health practitioners this might seem a reasonable baseline assumption to make, at the time it was a revolutionary departure from the norm.

Needing no further encouragement, plans were made for an overnight stay near the hospital in York. I surprised myself by eating the hearty English breakfast provided at our hotel, concentrating on small incidental things; pouring coffee and spreading marmalade on my toast, as though I belonged with the tourists and businessmen who made up the remainder of the clientele. Dave read the paper and made small talk, but I felt distanced from the everyday world, in a bubble from which there was no escape.

I was thankful for the proximity of The Retreat to our hotel - a short stroll past sedate Victorian mansions brought us to the entrance. Secluded from the road by well-tended gardens the outside of the building did not resemble the unforgiving mental health institutions of my imagination. Reminiscent of a country house hotel, this impression was retained on entering the elegant interior where we introduced ourselves at reception. Jane, the CEO, greeted us promptly and we were shown into a comfortable private room and offered refreshment.

'I've ordered lunch here, to give you plenty of time to read through your mother's file. I've also requested our counsellor Amy to join us later, as I'm sure you will have questions she may be able to help with.'

On the table lay a thick brown folder, the cover neatly handwritten; 'Andree Nada Sandgren – Retreat file, 30th June 1952 – 29th January 1958'. I was struck by how long the papers had lain untouched and how improbable it would have seemed to my mother if she had known that in fifty years' time her daughter would be reading them, laying bare the painful truth.

Shortly after my birth in the spring of 1952, just days after the air crash that killed her own mother, Nada suffered a mental breakdown and went to stay with her Godmother, Lady Playfair, in Edinburgh. The file began with a letter dated 30th July 1952 written by Professor Duncan at the Royal Edinburgh Infirmary, recommending Nada's admission to The Retreat. The letter continued:

'Nada has practically no friends or relatives, beyond her father who takes no notice of her, and Lady Playfair (her godmother). She struck me as an essentially nice and pleasant person whose psychological devastation is the result of appalling circumstances in her life rather than due to any inherent mental instability and feel she requires protection and rehabilitation rather than any deep psychological treatment. She has a horror of being left alone, and indeed is not in a fit state to be so. Her son is in a satisfactory home at present and her daughter is to be adopted, which causes Nada great mental distress. I feel she would be a very suitable case for The Retreat and that she would probably be a very pleasant patient whom it would be worthwhile to put on the rails again.'

On admission Nada was described as 'mildly asocial and depressed, reluctant to talk about herself. Although her conversation is free and logical there is a tendency to lying if the truth should show her in a bad light. She admits to not having been a good scholar despite being educated at the best schools. Currently recovering from an illness following the birth of her second child four months ago, she has been heard sobbing in the night and does not sleep well. Also lacks concentration and is restless – a not very intelligent, immature girl, erratic and unreliable.'

Nada's Godmother provided her own version:
'Nada went to good schools, but was expelled. She went to Elizabeth Arden's for a course on beauty culture. She met a Swedish man, and followed him to Sweden where she met and married her husband. She had a baby, but her husband was not the father. She had a breakdown whilst in Sweden and spent some time in a mental hospital where she was also treated for alcoholism. Her husband disappeared and left no address. Nada then had an affair with another man in Sweden, became pregnant and returned to England where the child was born. It is to be adopted. The patient has a considerable annual income from her father, and her mother was an heiress.'

Pages of medical notes detailed treatment; Doctor Torrie made regular observations:
11th August: 'It was suggested to Nada today that she might have been happier if she had less unearned income. She denied it and in view of her record of only mediocre scholarship it was felt that the patient might be of subnormal intelligence. A progressive matrix test failed to confirm this.'
13th August: 'The only line of approach appears to be to educate her to avoid the follies of her behaviour, rather than attempt to change her mode of life. She is so completely without conscience about her behaviour as to fail to see why she should not carry on as she has done previously.'
2nd September: 'It is felt that many things are beyond Nada's intellectual capacity. She still has no idea of what she intends to do in future except to find a 'good, steady man' to marry and found a home with.'
25th October: 'Nada's godmother Lady Playfair visited this afternoon after interviewing Nada's father and solicitor in London. Her father has now agreed that if Nada can remain well for six months then he will be pleased to have her to live with him in the USA. The patient was not terribly convinced by her father's proposal, however, saying he had made similar suggestions in the past, but never carried them through.'

A proposal for Nada's future was made by her solicitor John Rothwell-Dyson in October, perhaps with The Retreat in mind as a possible home: 'I have been talking to Mr Tevis following upon your letter of the 13th about future arrangements for his daughter's happiness and health. It appears that both of us think she is quite incapable of looking after a flat and her son on her own. The happiest solution would be if she could have her son with her, and do some paid work as well. Do you think Mrs Sandgren capable of working, unpaid, in some institution, where she could have her own quarters, and her child with her, and the little boy would thus have the benefit of having other people to look after him as well as his mother? I shall very much appreciate any suggestions you can make.'
Dr Torrie replied: 'The question of Mrs Sandgren's future remains a severe problem. I will be in London all next week, and it would be helpful if you could arrange a meeting with Mr Tevis. I feel more will be achieved at a personal discussion of the difficulties than through correspondence.'

Lady Playfair: 'I wonder how Nada is doing, and whether you have been able to persuade her to go into the convent at Whitby. She seemed rather restive when I saw her the other day, although I think a setback is only natural after the signing of the adoption papers for the second child. This is an enormously important hurdle negotiated, and must have taken its' toll of her. I did see her father in London, and although he says he will take no responsibility, in fact he is becoming willing to do so, and has discussed taking her abroad, even making the comment that she would have to be presented as his daughter. This is entirely new, as hitherto he has refused to think of her in this way. It is therefore very important that Nada should not blot her copy-book, but should return to the much-improved state of a month or so ago, although I suppose one cannot expect miracles.'

Nada to John Rothwell-Dyson: 'I received your letter last week, and am wondering if you saw my father on Wednesday as you said. I am still on this treatment of modified insulin, so am unable to go into town without a nurse although the doctor has said I may go in and collect my clothes from the cleaners. Every day here seems to drag when one is woken at 5.30 in the morning, and then there is nothing much to look forward to. I do hope I shall be able to see Hugh shortly, or at least some member of my family – I might just as well be in another country. I am so fed-up living like this and being ill.'

Doctor's notes, 18th November: 'I recently interviewed Mrs Sandgren's father in London. He is not prepared to take any responsibility for her other than financial and indeed seemed to be more concerned about her son than about her.'

Doctor Torrie to Nada's solicitor, 20th November: 'I am glad I had the opportunity of meeting yourself and Mr Tevis as many points were cleared up satisfactorily. On my return here Monday I found that Nada was much improved, and I have suggested to her that she goes for a week to the convent at Whitby, where she has friends. Hopefully the religious atmosphere may once again stir up the desire to become a nun.
I have discussed the matter of the child with my colleagues and it has been suggested that Stefan be made a Ward in Chancery. We realise that this will cause resistance, but feel that from the child's point of view, such a step is imperative. I hope you will be good enough to let me know your and Mr Tevis's reactions to this proposal.'

This idea was not taken up as Nada's solicitor wrote in early December: 'I saw Mr Tevis on Friday and he feels that there should now be some definite constructive policy for Nada. We both feel that we can only endeavour to fall in with whatever arrangements Nada wants. If Nada makes her own suggestions with your help, we will consider them most carefully and arrange for the payment of a monthly allowance which provides for Nada and her son. Mr Tevis is leaving for the States before Christmas, returning here late January and he does feel that as soon as the Christmas Season is over, that a move should be made for Nada. I should very much appreciate your suggestions.'

12th December from Nada's doctor to solicitor: 'As Mrs Sandgren has apparently indicated to you, she is becoming somewhat impatient here. Her proposal at the moment is to go to Edinburgh in order to be with her child at Christmas. She is hoping that Lady Playfair will invite her. It is difficult to obtain any decision about her future, but she tells me that her ultimate aim is to find someone to be a suitable father for her child, and marry him. She has made up her mind to return to Sweden next year, and there seems a danger of a recurrence of old problems. Her views as to her future change from day to day. I will inform you at once if she really comes to any practical solution or if she should decide to leave.'

14th December, John Rothwell Dyson: 'Mr Tevis has left for the United States and will not be back until the end of January. It is even more difficult for me to deal with this matter without his assistance. Mrs Sandgren seems to think that provided she has a regular monthly allowance she will manage to live on it, but I am afraid that we are all rather doubtful about this project.'

17th December, Dr Torrie: 'The present arrangements are as follows - Nada will spend Christmas in Edinburgh so as to be with her son and allow him to become used to her again. Afterwards they will both return here, and if she should appear incapable of caring for her son, I think that some further move should be made to prevent her from being responsible for him. I believe we have already suggested the possibility of a Ward in Chancery.

At the moment Nada is determined to return to Sweden in the spring or summer of 1953, and I believe has in mind the establishment of some liaison with one of her ex-lovers. This, of course, merely confirms my opinion that she is not sufficiently trustworthy to live a life without supervision.'

A letter from John Rothwell Dyson on the 20th December seemed to indicate that the idea of making Stefan a Ward in Chancery was becoming more attractive: 'I have received your letter of the 17th inst. and whereas I am extremely glad that there is a concrete proposal, I am a little worried on the financial side as I do not think Mr Tevis is prepared to increase the amount he pays for the upkeep of his daughter and her son. I think your suggestion as to the Ward in Chancery is an excellent one and must be considered in detail next year.'

Nada set off for Edinburgh on 22nd December 1952, with the intention of staying with her Godmother over Christmas, although the following day, Lady Playfair sent a discouraging telegram to Doctor Torrie: 'Unable to exercise any supervision of Mrs Sandgren over Christmas Season.'

28th December, Nada to Dr Torrie: 'This is just to let you know I shall be back on Tuesday unless you hear to the contrary. I should be grateful if you could arrange for a car to meet me, as I shall have Stefan's pram and clothes with me, but not little Stefan this time. For one thing, he has rather a nasty cold at present and I do not want to upset him while he is 'under the weather'. I propose coming back for him at the end of next month. I think if I bring his pram and clothes this time it will not mean so much next. Of course, he is not used to me yet, although I believe he remembers me very well, and now says "Mamma" when he sees me, is thrilled to have me back so he can play up! I do not feel up to coping with a screaming baby and loads of luggage at the same time! It is not exactly a short journey. I am enjoying myself in Edinburgh and it was lovely spending Xmas with my little son, he is so big now and well looking, and I am so pleased with him. My father sent Stefan a lovely Teddy Bear for Christmas, which he simply adores!'

Lady Playfair communicated her own version of events in a letter to Dr Torrie: 'In spite of my telegram, I did see Nada every day while she was in Edinburgh over Christmas and my husband and I had to admit that (apart from the claim on one's time that being kind to her inevitably entailed) she was really no trouble at all. She struck us as being a long way on the road to rehabilitation, and displayed self-confidence and self-respect quite new to her – also a far greater calmness and capacity in dealing with the practical problems of life.'
However, Lady Playfair expressed alarm that a new companion of Hugh's, Barbara Bramley, had taken on the responsibility of finding someone to look after Nada, whom she dismissed as 'some woman in the country who will have her for a time'. The letter continued: 'Miss Bramley was a friend of Nada's mother and is not well disposed towards Nada. She was a member of the pleasure party to South Africa and yet never wrote or communicated with Nada after the tragedy of her mother's death. It may be that I am prejudiced against Miss Bramley by the fact that the 'economy' in Nada's giving birth to the little girl in the East End Maternity hospital, in circumstances which I am sure must have had a bad effect on her psychologically, must be set off against the expense of taking Miss Bramley to South Africa on the most extravagant tour. I feel that any arrangements she makes will be with the same idea of economising on Nada so that there would be more for pleasure, which was always Elizabeth's policy, unfortunately. Miss Bramley is also 'very much on Hugh Tevis's doorstep' at present, and this is a factor which has to be reckoned with.'

6th January 1953, doctor's notes: 'Nada has settled down fairly well since readmission. Is now taking a more active part in social activities and has been persuaded to recommence occupational therapy.'

14th January 1953: 'Patient has remained stable with only one outburst of temper and no hysterical screaming. The question of the child joining her remains in abeyance.'

26th January: 'The provisional plan is that she should choose a furnished flat in either Edinburgh or London; secondly come here for a week or two with the child; thirdly settle herself with the child at the flat; fourthly undergo training and start work.'

Dr Torrie communicated this proposal to John Rothwell-Dyson the following day, and soon received a reply:

'Thank you for your letter, a copy of which I have sent to Nada's father. Do you really think that Nada is capable of running a flat on her own? As you have been more in touch with her recently than we have, I may be entirely wrong in thinking otherwise. I will discuss the matter with her father and advise you shortly.'

Hugh responded: 'I confirm our telephone conversation during which we agreed you would write to Dr Torrie in the following terms:

That both you and I are in accord with his general recommendations.

1. That in our opinion it would be best for Nada to try in the first instance to find a furnished flat in Edinburgh.

2. After having found suitable accommodation she should return to the Retreat for two or three weeks as recommended by Dr Torrie to enable her to pass through what he terms 'the transitional period of caring for her child.'

3. When she takes up residence with her child in the flat, she should find a suitable crèche and become trained in the occupation of choice.

4. That you inform Dr Torrie of the amount of Nada's annual income to enable him to help her frame a budget. In view of past experiences, I would consider it wise if this was paid in monthly instalments. It might even be prudent and helpful to Nada, once we know the amount of her rent, for the bank to be instructed to pay this prior to crediting her account with the balance available.

5. As I told you I shall be delighted to see Nada but doubt if this will be possible prior to my return from Southern Rhodesia early in March. In the meantime, I look forward to seeing you at lunch on Monday.'

While the men lunched, Lady Playfair abdicated responsibility; Professor Duncan of the Royal Infirmary Edinburgh informed Dr Torrie: 'Lady Playfair is very worried at the suggestion that Nada might be intending to live and work in Edinburgh. When Nada's mother died, Lady Playfair kindly took pity on the daughter in her great distress, and during her pregnancy gave her temporary refuge. Lady Playfair now feels that Hugh is attempting to shift all the responsibility for Nada's future on to her. All Nada's relations are in London – her own natural father who supports her, her two step-brothers and any friends she has. As her father seems to feel that his responsibility is liquidated after he has signed the cheque, it would seem to be much wiser for him to pay a competent woman to act as companion to Nada, and supervise her permanently. Lady Playfair and her husband, in spite of all their kindness to her in the past, firmly decline to undertake this supervision.'

5th February, Dr Torrie to John Rothwell-Dyson: 'I am in full agreement with all that you say in your letter about Nada. In any case she has now chosen to live in London rather than Edinburgh, so Lady Playfair need no longer be worried on that score. The position from our point of view is not quite so simple. Perhaps you do not know that her father was divorced from her mother when Nada was only a baby. From that time until she was twenty-two or three, he never saw her. Since this is the case, he has decided that he cannot be responsible for her any other way than financially. He has, however, made her a generous allowance. In addition, he spends at least half of his time outside England in America, Southern Rhodesia and South Africa, looking after his business interests. The difficulty, therefore, is not so much in realising she needs someone to be responsible for her, as to find someone who is willing to do so.'

3rd February, John Rothwell Dyson to Dr Torrie: 'Mr Tevis and I have given most careful consideration to your suggestions. We have an alternative suggestion and I wonder what you think of it – that is, that Nada should look for a flat in York and in consequence remain near you for advice.
There is one thing that Mr Tevis thinks would not be good for Nada and that is to take a flat in London with its' many temptations and lack of friendship, for she really does not have any friends here now.
The question of income needs to be stressed because the current demands are, of course, completely out of keeping with her income and it should be made clear to Nada that Mr Tevis will not continue at this rate.
I have only one other comment to make. It seems to me it would take a very strong-minded young woman to manage the flat, drop her child to a crèche in the morning, work all day and then call for the child in the evening and return to a solitary life without a husband.'

Dr Torrie: 'I am afraid that the prospect of a flat in York does not appeal to Nada, and in any case, I expect to be leaving York in the not too distant future and know that the restraining influence of The Retreat is dependent upon her attachment to me.
We have received a letter from Professor Duncan at Edinburgh Royal Infirmary, expressing in no uncertain terms Lady Playfair's unwillingness to accept responsibility for her.
If only a satisfactory companion, acceptable to both sides, could be found, I feel that our troubles would be minimized. I believe you had someone in mind. In any case I feel that it is only fair that Nada should now be given a chance to prove herself. If she stays at The Retreat for too long, she will become so dependent on others that permanent institutional care may be needed. I would therefore stress the importance of getting her on the road back to normality as a matter of urgency.'

12th February, John Rothwell Dyson: 'Many thanks for your letter which I was able to discuss with Mr Tevis before he left for Rhodesia. We fully appreciate your views and obviously there is now nothing to be done but to arrange for Nada to come to London. My secretary and several other people are now going to work to see what they can do and perhaps you will kindly tell Nada that we are not neglecting her and hope to give her some news before long.'

13th February, Dr Torrie: 'Unfortunately we are unable to legally insist on Nada being supervised. Nada has again brought up the subject of her return to Sweden, and this should be combated. I think that it is a pity we cannot get together in an endeavour to find some satisfactory solution, but I am afraid that such a meeting must be postponed for the time being.'

17th February, John Rothwell Dyson: 'I have had a preliminary interview with a prospective companion for Nada this morning and am going to see her flat this afternoon. If the arrangement materialises, I think it will be all we could hope for.
I do agree that at all costs Nada must be prevented from going to Sweden.'

Medical notes 25th February: 'Mrs Sandgren has been drinking again in town. She did not settle on return and is spending the night in a side room. Town parole cancelled.'

3rd March: 'Nada remains tense. She is to go to London tomorrow to meet the proposed companion and may stay over until next week to see a friend returning from South Africa to Sweden. She expresses dissatisfaction at the prospect of having to have a companion but will possibly accept this rather than stay here. She is not certifiable.'

5th March: 'Nada left hospital very reluctantly this morning to catch the train to London.'

8th March: 'Nada returned today after having a terrific row with her solicitor. She did, however, meet the companion and found they got on quite amicably together.'

19th March: 'Nada has remained quite well during the past few days and although apprehensive about living in London she accepts that the longer she puts it off the more difficult it will be. Nada was discharged today to my great relief.'

Nada wrote Dr Torrie a letter dated 8th April 1953 describing her flat hunting experiences in London: 'I have been going to Estate Agents but have nothing concrete so far. However, this is only just the beginning! If I can get such a thing as an unfurnished flat in the Hampstead area, my father will help me furnish it.'

'My Dear Doctor,   London 22nd April

I went to the flat yesterday, which now is mine. Of course, it's not at all in order yet, but even at the moment I can see the foreshadowing of great change! Furnishing it is very exciting – my father has evidently changed his mind, as he has told me to get what I like and put it down to him, but that he wants no part in helping me choose the antiques. However maybe I can manage even this on my own! I shall be interested to know what you think of it when I have finished.'

'My Dear Doctor,   29th April

I have been very busy so far this week, as I am now buying furniture for the flat! This has proved to be very exciting and rather tiring, as you may imagine!

We spent the day at Maples yesterday, and are due to spend another on Friday. By that time, I should have everything done, with the exception of a few details. I went out to dinner with my father last Thursday, and he is giving me some help after all, which is very nice.

London is absolute hell just now what with the 'milling millions' who have come down to see the Coronation. At least I shall be out of the way – I am going to Sweden on the 19th May for a month. Don't worry about me, I feel free at last. Many thanks are due to you, the fact that I feel as I do today. Write and tell me you're pleased; it would help a lot. I only think of the future now, which you told me once, is all that matters.'

Nada journeyed to Sweden during the summer of 1953, as planned. The British Consulate General in Gothenburg wrote to John Rothwell Dyson in August:

.... 'I regret to have to report that after all arrangements had been made for Mrs Sandgren's journey to London, she refused at the last moment to leave the hospital where she is being cared for.

The Superintendent at St. Jorgen's hospital is at a loss to know what to do next. His patient is not in need of hospital treatment and he wishes her to leave as soon as possible. He is of the opinion that she has become institutionally minded, hence her reluctance to leave.

It does occur to me that Mrs Sandgren must surely have some close relative who has influence over her and who might consider coming out to Gothenburg and talk her over to a more reasonable frame of mind or at least install in her a sense of responsibility towards her child in Scotland.'

Dr Bjornberg, St. Jorgen's hospital, 11th September 1953: 'It seems impossible to bring her back to England. When the journey is imminent, she immediately shows hysterical reactions which make her compulsory discharge impossible. I hope that I can a find a place for her to live here in Sweden.'

8th January, 1954: 'This young woman has no possibility to take care of herself and having serious suicidal tendencies, she is certifiable here in Sweden. Now she wants to go back to England but for how long time she will be of this opinion is impossible to know. I hope that this wish will last so long time that we can manage the journey and bring her to leave Gothenburg for London.
It will be the best that a nurse follows her to London and I think it would be the best that you take care of Mrs Sandgren at the Retreat.'

Dr Torrie quashed these plans, writing on the 13th January 1954: 'Permanent supervision in an institution under our Mental Treatment Act is not possible.'

Sweden 14th January 1954, Nada to her solicitor:
'Dear John,
I received your letter and was very pleased to hear Stefan had got his tricycle alright, also that Kate (Playfair) had bought him something, and Hugh too.
I have now 106 Kroner and I would be grateful if you would send me some more money as soon as possible, as I must get a winter coat and shoes for when I come away from the hospital. I am borrowing while I am here. Dr Bjornberg has said I can go to England on the 23rd of this month so I must get something warm for the journey. I must save the money I have to pay the bill for my treatment. Luckily it is very cheap here, and the treatment has been excellent.
As to my future, I'm afraid the way does not lie straight before me. My own future of course, is empty and completely negative, but now I am thinking only of Stefan. Where I shall make my home, and what I shall do is not at all clear in my mind. If I am to live alone with my son, then it must be in my own country. If I should marry again then of course it is another story. Honestly, John, I think marriage is the best solution, and I have a chance, but I shall speak about that another time. Now I want to come to England, wait a while and see how I feel. I think it is the thing that may help me forget the ache in my heart, as time doesn't seem to do much. Making a home for Stefan will be wonderful. I have felt so terribly apathetic about things for so long that I don't understand myself – occasionally I get a burst of enthusiasm and then again, the same old apathy, back it comes to stay!
Anyway, John, thank you for what you've done for me in every respect.'

On January 19th Dr Torrie wrote to John Rothwell Dyson: 'The question of adoption must be proceeded with and presumably we can rely upon you to support an application to the Court, if necessary, as the mother is obviously incapable of looking after her son.' In a letter dated 20th January he wrote 'It is clear we cannot now admit Mrs Sandgren unless she comes under certification. We are willing to support an application for the adoption of the child on the grounds of the mental incapacity of the mother, after we have seen her again.'

John Rothwell Dyson notified Dr Torrie that 'We have arranged accommodation in London for two days. Mrs Sandgren will be accompanied by a sister from the hospital who will take her to The Retreat as we presume you have already made these arrangements with the Swedish hospital. Please confirm.'

Dr Torrie: 'With reference to our telephone conversation yesterday, after full consultation with all the specialists who handled Nada in the Retreat, we are firmly of the opinion that certification is necessary before her return here.

When she arrives in London on Monday, she should be taken to one of the private clinics such as the York Clinic, Guys Hospital, where they can observe her.'

The file held one final letter from John Rothwell Dyson, dated 26th January: 'I shall be seeing Nada today and we are naturally most exercised in our minds as to where she shall go.'

Thus, the vexed question of Nada's future was held in abeyance, providing no hint of the decision that must eventually have been reached, for the pages ended here. It appeared Nada had never returned to The Retreat but continued her lonely and remorseless downward spiral, perceived as a burden to be passed from one authority to the next, one friend or relative to another. Was she the orchestrator of her fate? Most certainly; in the same way a sleepwalker is to blame for falling through a window.

Dave and I left The Retreat amidst tears and promises to keep in touch, the late sun slipping behind the trees as we made our way aimlessly into the city, the days' revelations lying heavy as a badly digested meal. Strolling aimlessly through the early evening streets we found ourselves at the door of the cathedral, open to us as they have been to countless others over the millennia. Taking one of the votive candles I placed the flickering light at the altar, drawing comfort from the single flame merging into the blaze of hundreds more.

*

On our return home, we discovered Ian had not returned from a trip to Euro-Disney with friends. His mobile went straight to voice mail. I didn't know these friends of his, just that they worked together part time, selling advertising space for the same company. We drove to their offices and cajoled an employee into giving us the land line number of a colleague; I felt a surge of relief when a woman answered,
"I'm worried too. They've never been this late back before".
"I didn't know they'd been to Euro-Disney before."
"Euro-Disney? You think they've been to Euro Disney?"
Silence.
"They're in Amsterdam…." another pause "…… for the drugs. They all do it. Smoke weed and stuff. I'm sorry you didn't know; it must be a shock."
But it wasn't a shock, not really. We could deceive ourselves no longer. It all fitted. It wasn't a shock at all, just another piece of self-deception hitting the rails.
By this time Ian was on a ferry heading for Dover, and called us. "You're grounded" Dave announced grimly, "and if you're carrying any stuff on you, for God's sake throw it overboard!"
If only we could have jettisoned our anxieties as easily.
Immersed in the repercussions from Ian's return, it took me a few days to recollect that I had heard nothing from Stefan. I knew he was in Chicago for a few days on business but by Friday, convinced something was wrong, phoned his office. Carla answered the call, her voice cautious.
"Hi Carla, how are you?"
"Oh, I'm OK," a slight stress on the 'I'.
"I haven't heard from Stefan ………is he still in Chicago?"
"He's not in Chicago, Diane …." her voice sounded weary, "he admitted himself to a clinic. There's no easy way to tell you this, he's an addict, and he's been in and out of rehab for years, for most of his adult life. That's where he is now, and I have to hope it will work this time, but it never has before, so why should I think this time will be any different……"
Carla described the toxic effect of Stefan's addiction on their family life, money wasted on parties at expensive hotels, where he enjoyed supplying 'friends' with drugs, drink and girls.

Such binges were followed by remorse and admittance to rehab, the pattern repeated over and over.

I must have sounded unbelievably naïve from Carla's world-weary viewpoint as I attempted to reassure, whilst knowing she was being tested to the limit of endurance by Stefan's continual relapses. I wondered, silently, why she had ever thought marriage and a child a reasonable enterprise with him. In Carla's words, "I just want my husband back, the husband I married. I know you must think I was too hasty, that I didn't really know him, but when Stefan asked to marry me, I felt like a princess in a fairy tale. Everything was perfect. We married on Valentine's Day and it was the happiest day of my life, Stefan cried in my arms on our wedding night.... he said he was so lucky to have found me. He said we'd always be happy together........I'm tired, Diane, so tired of it all. If love can't save someone like Stefan, then what's the point of my religion...... or of anything at all?"

I searched desperately to find the right words, something sincere, not trite or cliché-ridden, yet found myself repeating "I'm so sorry," as though I were in some way to blame. The dream I treasured of the perfect all-American family, wholesome as apple pie in their pretty house behind the white picket fence, was after all only a mirage.

Despite evidence to the contrary, I determined on a positive approach and persuaded myself that Stefan's stay in rehab had been a success. Now in possession of a green card, Stefan and Carla planned to fly to the UK immediately after Christmas. There was only a short time to manage a whole host of preparations. While my thoughts and energies were thus taken up, another cloud gathered on the horizon.

Throughout November there was a remorseless decline in dad's health. The slow accumulation of symptoms, at one time seeming under control, now gathered pace. He preferred to sit in the half light, the curtains partially drawn shutting out the meagre dose of daylight afforded at that gloomy time of year while he reminisced about the past. I began to wonder, during those hours when he seemed entirely to forget my presence, if he would step into that long-forbidden territory, but he did not. I could not fail to notice his increasing stillness, the absent look in his eyes. Despite the best efforts of his GP, hospital admission became inevitable.

One Saturday evening Sarah decided she wanted to visit her granddad after I had already spent a long afternoon at his bedside and was reluctant to go back. Sarah would not be thwarted, her intensity of purpose finally persuading me. My warning that she would find him in a very much worse condition seemed overplayed when we entered the ward and saw he was awake, a little less drawn, and quite coherent. We spoke of inconsequential things, and he was clearly delighted at our unplanned visit. As we were leaving, he said goodnight, and told Sarah he loved her.

It should not have come as a surprise when the phone rang in the early hours. I did not get back to the hospital in time, he had already slipped away.

Among my father's papers I found he had left me all the adoption documents, together with a form already filled in, to apply for a copy of my original, full birth certificate. It seemed he wanted to unburden himself of the secret after all. His part in the story was over, but from beyond the grave he had bestowed permission for me to continue with mine.

~~~~~~~~~~~~~~~~~~~~~~~~~~~~~~~~~~~~~

A long out of print book 'The Ponsonby Family', which had once graced the shelves of the University of San Diego library, was currently advertised online by a second-hand bookseller. The 1929 edition was 'in fair condition with damaged cover and binding', which seemed of small moment to me, excited by the idea of finding a history of my maternal grandmother's family in a single volume, without having to hunt down all the information myself. The volume did not disappoint, although unsurprisingly perhaps, the printed family tree showed the union between Elizabeth Prudence Ponsonby and Hugh Tevis as childless.

In the preface, written by no less a personage than Major-General Sir John Ponsonby, of Haile Hall, he writes that he has included the dull members of the family as well as the more notable ones who distinguished themselves as politicians, soldiers, sailors and diplomats. He added that in every walk of life 'the family seem to have taken their own line and to have acted according to their convictions without regard to consequences.' Amen to that.

As far as my own tastes are concerned, a volume of family history has little appeal unless the narrative provides an insight into everyday lives and concerns. Certainly, my curiosity was aroused by reading that a certain John Ponsonby, who lived in the time of King Henry II, was fined 'because he wanted pledges', and that another John, in the year 1393 'that without special licence of the King, he shall not depart to any foreign parts, nor make nor cause to be made any suit or attempt which may tend to contempt or prejudice of the king'.

A visit to Cumbria, particularly Haile Hall and the village of Ponsonby, was initiated by intriguing snippets such as these. I was disappointed that Haile Hall could not be seen from any vantage point along the road, being situated some considerable distance past a gatehouse. Pausing to take photographs, I experienced much the same feelings of an interloper lacking credentials as I had years previously standing on the pavement outside my mother's old home in Knightsbridge Village.

Adjourning to the graveyard of Haile Church, where some of the more illustrious members of the Ponsonby family are interred in ornate tombs it is nevertheless a memorial leaning against the wall of the church in somewhat neglected fashion that I shall remember:

'Learn reader, under this stone doth lye,
a rare example cald John Ponsonbye,
If I said any lese, I'm sure I lyed,
He was a faithfull freind and soe he dyd.
November 25 in the year 1670'

A somewhat enigmatic epitaph, which stills stirs my curiosity; I would have liked to know more about this particular John Ponsonby, and the friend who saw fit to have the memorial carved. But alas, John is a name which occurs with confusing frequency within the family, and as no records survive of a death in 1670, the identity of John and the friend to whom he had been so faithful, remain a mystery.

~~~~~~~~~~~~~~~~~~~~~~~~~~~~~~~~~~~~~~~

The Tevis family history should have been an altogether easier proposition as my brother Stefan, brought up by our maternal grandfather, Hugh Tevis, had already provided books, photographs and documents. Yet I found that prolific facts and figures about the Tevis business empire could not fill the gap left by a lack of personal papers, letters or diaries. Stefan had found our grandfather Hugh a distant and uncommunicative figure and this aura of impenetrability seeped into every Tevis ancestor I tried to illuminate, even Hugh's grandfather Lloyd, about whom a great deal has been written. **See Appendix 2**

Lloyd Tevis remains an enigmatic figure; romantic hero or robber baron depending on one's point of view. From the angle of his business career, he was clearly a successful man, building a multi-million-dollar empire from relatively humble beginnings. But learning about these accomplishments provides a one-dimensional picture, and tells nothing of Lloyd's personality or character. As one of California's earliest pioneers, he no doubt fulfilled that purpose of 'a colonist, explorer, settler of new land, and innovator', yet still left me to wonder what matters were of concern to him as he returned each night to his palatial home on Nob Hill, where he was described as hosting lavish parties and entertainments, and where, according to one newspaper his wife wore 'the largest diamond ever seen in San Francisco'. Did he have an overbearing presence; an inflated view of his own importance? Dubious dealings in partnership with James Ben Ali Haggin as Kern Land Holdings, where by devious means water rights were acquired, and poor settlers turned off their land suggest a cold, calculating, grasping desire for wealth at any cost and there is little evidence of any philanthropic gestures.

The vast inheritance passed down to his children and grandchildren must have warped their view of the world, as evidenced by a mural painted in imitation of Michaelango's 'The Creation of Man', starring grandfather Hugh in the role of Creator. Latterly a house was named 'Caesar's Palace' – without any humorous intent. Yet my brother Stefan had spoken of our grandfather's philanthropy and generosity, and the remote Lloyd Tevis as a hero worthy of admiration. In the hope of some answers, I travelled with my husband, brother and a friend to America's West Coast, on the trail of these shadowy ancestors.

We began at the Wells Fargo headquarters in Montgomery Street, on the same site Wells Fargo first opened for business in 1852, and where Lloyd was president for twenty years from 1872 to 1892.

We couldn't resist squeezing inside an original Wells Fargo stagecoach dating from 1858, the four of us seeming to fill the whole of the available space and were amazed that it was designed to accommodate up to nine people – with a further nine on top. It must have been an incredibly arduous journey when the time taken to travel from St. Joseph Missouri to San Francisco was twenty-one days and nights.

Stefan had arranged for us to meet Bill and Marianne, the Wells Fargo Museum archivist and Vice President, and they had already raided the archives for newspaper articles, photographs and original papers.

Some of the story was already known to me; that Lloyd studied law under his father Samuel Tevis, an attorney in Kentucky, and tried various employments before joining the California gold rush in May of 1849 as one of the original 49ers. He set up camp in an area known as Dry Diggins. This gold camp sprang up in the space of a few months along a canyon creek in El Dorado County. A place lacking any law enforcement agency or criminal justice system in these early days, it became known as Hangtown creek after townspeople took the law into their own hands, and hung some men from an oak tree. The oak tree stump still exists under the floor of the saloon called the Hangman's Tree.

After building a single room cabin to live in Lloyd set to work in the placers, but nine months later was no closer to finding a fortune. He made the decision to return to Sacramento where he knew there would be plenty of business opportunities in the rapidly expanding cities of the West.

He was joined by his older brother Robert, who had also trained as a lawyer. Robert, described as excitable, hot-headed and of fierce courage, with Southern notions of chivalry and honour, was killed in July 1855, shot through the heart in a duel, after an argument over politics prompted by a speech he gave. There was nothing to indicate how Lloyd was affected by his brother's death, but one could only imagine the huge impact it must have made.

In Sacramento Lloyd was able to save some salary which he used to purchase a piece of land for $250. Within a short while he set up what was to become a famed partnership with an old school friend of Turkish descent – James Ben Ali Haggin. The two men became lifelong partners, and their friendship was cemented by their marrying sisters, both daughters of Colonel Lewis Sanders, also from Kentucky.

It was during these years that Lloyd built up extensive land holdings – the Kern County Land Company, co-owned with James Haggin, comprising a third of a million acres in the San Joaquin Valley. By 1853 Lloyd had moved his home to San Francisco, where his business interests ranged from shipping to lighting gas, dry docks to ice companies, and most importantly gold and silver mines in California, Utah, Nevada, Idaho, and the Anaconda mine in Montana. Lloyd was president of Southern Pacific railroad from 1869-1870, and a founding member of Pacific Coast Oil Co, eventually Chevron Corp. In addition, he was a major stockholder in Spring Valley Water Company, Risdon Iron Works and Sutro Tunnel at Virginia City, Nevada. When gold was found in the Black Hills, Lloyd, James Ben Ali Haggin and George Hearst purchased the famous Homestake mine in South Dakota. Their partnership, Hearst, Haggin, Tevis and Co., soon became the largest mining concern in the world. Just two months before his death in 1899, Lloyd received $8 million for the sale of his share of The Anaconda copper mine in Nevada to a syndicate headed by J. D. Rockefeller.

In 1860 Tevis and Haggin acquired the Rancho del Paso property, where Lloyd lived for a time. In the1880s Haggin began to breed racehorses at the ranch. A total of 600 horses were kept in twenty-four stables each holding sixty-four stalls. Some were famous winners - Waterboy, Africander, Yellow Tail and Irish Lad. James's horse Ben Ali won the Kentucky Derby in 1886. Meanwhile, the Central Pacific Railroad was being built, which would eventually succeed the Wells Fargo Overland Mail. Lloyd was instrumental in organising Pacific Express to take over the express business on the line, thus weakening the position of Wells Fargo, whose stocks declined from $100 to $13 a dollar a share, at which point Lloyd made a substantial purchase. This led to him being in a position to take over Wells Fargo when his own Pacific Express Company entered into an exclusive ten-year agreement with Central Pacific railroad, for the carrying of mail. The signing of the Treaty of Omaha sealed the deal. Lloyd became president of Wells Fargo on February 8th 1872, a position he held for twenty years, thus becoming the longest serving president in the company's history.

By 1881 Lloyd's active involvement with wide ranging business interests was such, that he was invited by the American Bankers' Association to address their convention held on August 10th at Niagara Falls, on the subject of past and future growth of the industrial and banking system in California. During his address he made reference to the causes of 'boom and bust', and it should come as no surprise, perhaps, that the concern of inflation, fuelled by speculation and unsustainable growth, are the same problems we continue to face today.

Could he have seen into the future, he would have found his words possessed a prophetic quality, 'it is apparent that California's most valuable industries of the future will be that of the vineyard and orchard. California is by nature, the France of America.'

Hoping to find some insight into Lloyd's character and personality, I turned to the Gertrude Bell (1868-1926) letters – written by a lady who obtained a first-class history degree from Oxford University at a time when very few women received a university education. Subsequently travelling extensively, Gertrude recorded her experiences in both diaries and letters. One letter, dated 14th February 1898, contains a cameo of her meeting with Lloyd:

'When we returned to our inn, we found Mr. Tevis and his son (Hugh Tevis) waiting for us. He is the dearest old man. He came to San Francisco 48 years ago when it was a heap of sand and is full of interesting tales of adventure. He said it was he who advised Lisa's brother to go to the Klondike, that there was no risk, that was how he had laid the foundations of his fortune, and it was the right way to begin.' - it amused me to find that Lloyd was not immune to a little fanciful rewriting of history, when recounting his early life to this young lady.

The letter continued - 'We made many plans with him and departed at dinner time………we went to Mr Tevis' house for tea meeting him halfway up. There we found the good Mrs. Tevis and a charming little granddaughter. We came back just in time to dress and go out to dine at the University Club with Mr Hugh Tevis – the best dinner I have ever eaten and extremely merry. He too seems to have done every sort of thing and lived in every kind of place - he was extremely agreeable. I came away with an enormous bouquet of Californian violets. We all three went to a music hall and came back to our hotel for cold drinks. We parted the best of friends with an invitation to come and stay on the Tevis' Ranch, which we will certainly do some day. On Saturday Maurice took our luggage down to the ship. I went at 11a.m. to see Mr Tevis at his office which is in an enormous building close to the hotel. He took me all over – it is a marvellous place. "This building" he said "is made with as much delicacy and precision as the inside of a watch" – and so it was. We then went out to an immense provision store – built and run by himself – where I bought some tea and was shown all round and given strange fruits to eat. Besides this he owns two ranches, one 500 miles square, a copper mine, a gold mine, iron works, and probably many other things – these were all I happened to hear of. He is a hale and hearty old man, has never had a day's illness and takes all these things in his stride quite as a matter of course. It is a wonderful country. I am quite overcome by the vitality, energy and enterprise of it all. We were dreadfully sorry to leave….'

Likewise, we were sorry to take our leave of the Wells Fargo Museum, but soon forgot any lingering regrets on the stunning pacific highway to Sausalito and Monterey, the site of another Tevis family home, that of Lloyd's son Hugh. **See Appendix 3.**

Hugh was destined to never live in this house, built as a summer home for his young bride Cornelia Baxter, in 1901, and named 'Casa del Las Olas' (House of the Waves). Monterey was chosen as the location because it was where he had spent his summers from a child, at the lavish Hotel Del Monte which became the Tevis family's official summer residence and where they entertained in style for many years. Advertised as the most elegant seaside resort in the world, its' guests included presidents, kings, film stars and business magnates. The 7,000 acre Del Monte Forest and 17-Mile Drive, which optimized the most picturesque spots along the Monterey coast, like Cypress Point and Pebble Beach, were added to the original 126 landscaped acres, and soon guests could sample a glass-roofed swimming pavilion, racetrack, lake, tennis courts, and the Del Monte Golf Course.

MISS ALICE BOALT TEVIS

It was at the Hotel Del Monte that Hugh met both his future brides. The first, Alice Boalt, was the only daughter of Judge John H. Boalt. The wedding ceremony took place at 8:30pm on the 15th November 1890, at Grace Church, California Street, San Francisco. A report at the time described the bride as noted for her simple unassuming manners and accomplishments of a high order; Hugh was a popular young society gentleman employed in financial operations. The church was decorated with '13,000 chrysanthemums, columns of La France roses suspended between the chandeliers, and begonias and palms along the sides. The altar rail was also decorated with Jacqueminot and La Reine roses, violets and ferns with a centrepiece of lilies tied with white satin ribbon.'

Tragically Alice died suddenly of a heart attack while the couple were in New York in 1894. She was only twenty-four years old, and left her husband with a two-year-old daughter. Hugh spent as much time as possible with his young daughter, also named Alice, and it was she who introduced him to Cornelia McGhee Baxter **(see Appendix 4)**. Alice told her father, "You have to meet her Daddy. She looks like a princess." Hugh must have agreed, as he soon proposed marriage despite the fact that Cornelia was already engaged and planning her wedding when they met. The couple married just three weeks later, on 10th April, 1901.

"Casa del Las Olas" stretching for 1,000 feet along the waterfront was doomed never to become a family home for the newlyweds as tragedy struck during their round the world honeymoon cruise. While in Yokohama, Japan, where they were purchasing furnishings for the new house, Hugh became ill with appendicitis. He died on the 6th June 1901, just two months after they were married, after an attempt to operate was unsuccessful.
Thereby he was spared witnessing the death of his beloved daughter Alice just two years later, from Bright's disease.

Cornelia was left a widow aged only eighteen and already expecting a baby.
Cornelia moved into 'Casa del Las Olas' for a time, and her son, named Hugh after his father, was born there in February 1902. The house was sold the following year. Little could they have guessed that the beautiful house on Ocean View Avenue, with a thousand-foot ocean frontage and private beach would subsequently be sold to the sardine canning industry, and demolished in 1944 at the peak of wartime cannery production, by which time the whole area had become the epicentre of a huge fish processing industry. Ocean View Avenue was the real life setting of John Steinbeck's novel Cannery Row, in honour of which the road was eventually re-named.
It is still possible to imagine something of the elegance of the original house as photographs of the Tevis Estate were used in the planning and design of the Monterey Plaza Hotel and Spa, which currently occupies the site.

Appendix 1
William Rundall Ponsonby 11/8/1876 – 18/1/1919

Photo of (left to right) William and his brothers Reginald and George Montagu, their mother Lily noted on the reverse side 'Our dear boys, Willie, Reg, Montie'.

William (known as Willie or Tony) was the son of Colonel Justinian Gordon Ponsonby (known as Gordon), and Elizabeth Sophia Ponsonby (known as Lily), who were first cousins. His father was at one time Military Attaché to the Embassy at Constantinople. The family moved to where ever Justinian was stationed, and William spent some idyllic years in Bermuda with his family while his father served as Brigade Major there.

Justinian, Lily and their children pictured in Bermuda C. 1885.

William was the second of eight children, one of whom died in infancy, born to the couple. His father preferred the boys (there were five all told) to be educated at different schools, and William is recorded at Sedbergh, Cumbria for just one year from 1890 – 1891 and subsequently attended Philberts School in Maidenhead, Berkshire. After his mother, Lily died, early in 1890, her seven children were farmed out to various relatives during the holidays, and were never again to spend any time together under the same roof. It is unclear what motivated their father to take this action, certainly not heartbreak after the death of his wife, as he soon married again. His bride was Blanche Cook, sixteen years his junior. Her parents were horrified when they discovered that Justinian already had a family of seven, and insisted that Blanche was not to be responsible for the existing family. Blanche and Gordon would eventually have six children together.

William was enterprising and ambitious, with an adventurous spirit, and it is said that he ran away to sea, firstly signing up as a cadet on HMS Worcester.
William kept in touch with his siblings, as some letters to his sister Olive have survived. Just before Christmas 1894 he recounted events from his life at sea: "Terrible storm at sea not far from Cape Le Hague." (Normandy) "Captain told us to pray if we knew how. The 1st Mate saw a narrow channel marked in the chart and said if men would obey him he would try and get the ship through. Success!"
"We picked up 3 men on a spar. I have not had any sleep for 3 days. Everything is soaked, the water is pouring off me. The 1st Mate is an awfully nice man and is letting me write this in his cabin."

By February 1897 he was working for the New Zealand Shipping Company where he reached the rank of Second Mate. William must have missed his brothers and sisters as he wrote wistfully in 1897 from Wellington NZ:

"It is a long time since I saw you, isn't it? You must have changed a lot; I wonder if I would recognise you again. I don't think I have changed much except that I am a bit older looking and I suppose a bit rougher in my manners like most sailors."

Soon after this he joined the New South Wales mounted police from 1897-1899. When war broke out with the Boers in South Africa, in 1899, he decided to try his luck there. En route between Australia and Natal a letter home described his enjoyment of time spent in Australia, in Sydney and Melbourne, with parties and theatre trips, and how nearly all his money had been spent.

On arrival in South Africa William enlisted with Thorneycroft's mounted infantry on the 5th November 1899. Perhaps this irregular force appealed to his adventurous nature more than the regular army. A letter home described the harsh conditions: "We have been wandering about this desert for about six weeks now chasing a command of Boers (who will not stop and fight) and strewing dead horses and mules in our wake by the hundreds, living on whatever we can find and generally having a poor time of it. Ostrich eggs are the only thing we've been able to get recently and though they make a good feed and are very good once in a way, one gets deadly sick of them."

William was promoted to Lieutenant on the 10th December 1899 and to Captain on the 18th December 1900. For his bravery in rescuing a fallen comrade from the battlefield of Spion Cop on the 15th December 1899, when he was wounded, but fought on, he was awarded the DSO medal with six clasps. He fought at the following campaigns in South Africa: Cape Colony, Orange Free State, Transvaal, Tugela Heights, Relief of Ladysmith and Laing's Nek. In a letter written on the 31st December 1899 to daughter Olive, William's father expresses pride in his son: "Do you see how splendidly Willie has been behaving? All the newspapers mention him for his exceptional bravery and I shall be very much surprised if he is not recommended for the Victoria Cross – many a gallant fellow has received it for less"

A news report in the Natal Witness, 22nd December 1899 recounted events:

"Thorneycroft's provided a hero in the person of Lt. Ponsonby, of D Troop, who when his section was recalled, on account of the heavy fire remained behind with a wounded man, whose wounds he dressed. Then he tried to carry the man to safety. Whilst so engaged his helmet was pierced with a bullet, but he stuck with his task and moved forward with his burden. The injured man's life was , however, short, as while being carried a bullet lodged in his stomach, causing almost instant death.. The dying man's movements when writhing on the ground drew fresh fire and Ponsonby sought shelter for a short time. He then pushed on, receiving a flesh would on the left arm, while his coat was perforated. Noticing his condition, a Boer advanced to 80 metres to make sure of his victim, but Ponsonby drew his revolver, and shot him dead. When he returned to camp he received a well merited ovation from his friends. Later on, our hero went back to the fighting line, and again succoured a wounded comrade, this time saving him."

William wrote to his sister Olive in typically understated mode: "I am now laid on the shelf for a few weeks, worse luck – as I was shot through the arm at Colenso ...... nothing serious but very awkward as it happens to be my bridle arm. I wouldn't mind a bit if it was the other."

By April 1900 he was sufficiently recovered to continue fighting, his letter home stating:

"I got up again from the sick lines in time for the Monte Cristo fight and the relief of Ladysmith."

Newcastle Morning Herald, February 1900

During February 1900, the remnants of Thorneycroft's were fighting to relieve Ladysmith, and William continued alongside them until April 1901, when he joined the South African Constabulary.'

During the winter of 1901, William's brother Montie (George Montagu) died in a hunting accident in Northern Nigeria, where he was serving with the West African Frontier Force. He was out shooting duck, when the gun went off accidentally. The shot passed through his foot and caused an infection that the medics were powerless to overcome, and died a few days later. William wrote to his sister from Hoopsted:
"It is shocking bad luck old Montie pegging out from a shot in the foot, isn't it? When so many fellows get hit in the lungs and through the head etc and pull through."

In a letter dated 22nd February, 1902 and addressed to Major Vaughan, his officer in command of the South African Constabulary, William requested a recommendation for a Captains' commission in the regular army. Major Vaughan complied, sending the following message to Major General Baden-Powell on 23rd February, from Hoopstad:
'Forwarded and recommended. Captain Ponsonby is a capable and very dashing officer – quick to perceive opportunities in the field and ready to take advantage of them without delay.'
From Johannesburg, dated 3rd March 1902, Baden-Powell wrote:
'Sir, I have the honour to forward and recommend herewith for the favourable consideration of the Commander-in-chief, the application of Captain W. R. Ponsonby, South African Constabulary, for a Captain's Commission in one of His Majesty's Regiments of the Line,
I have the honour to be, Sir,

Your obedient Servant
Baden-Powell, Major General,
Inspector General, South African Constabulary.'

Despite the support of his commanding officers, there was a problem, and William wrote again on 4th April 1902:

'I note reply of the Military Secretary that the War Office has not definitely ruled that no commissions above the rank of 2nd Lieutenant be given – an application for a Captain's Commission was recommended and forwarded on my behalf to the war office by Major General Baden-Powell, since which date several Captain's commissions have been gazetted. My application must therefore have been received at the War Office before the present rule came into force – and I have the honour to request that as no reply to my first application has been made by the War Office, that this application may still be forwarded.'

As though to add weight to this request, Colonel Thorneycroft sent the following letter to the Military Secretary to the Commander in Chief, South Africa on the 15th April 1902:

'Sir,

With reference to the application of Capt. W.R. Ponsonby D.S.O. South African Constabulary, for a commission as Captain in the Regular Cavalry. I have the honour to bring to notice that this officer served in Thorneycroft's Mounted Infantry under my command for eighteen months with great distinction – he is a thoroughly good leader of men, and I have a very high opinion of his capabilities – and trust that his application may be favourably considered. His first application, which was made before the present regulations were in force appears to have been lost – and I think that it would be a great pity if his services to the State were lost on this account as I am sure that he would make a good cavalry officer, for which position he is professionally, socially and financially fitted.

I have the honour to be sir

Your obedient servant,

Guy Thorneycroft,

Colonel.'

On a page of notepaper dated 12th June 1902 the Military Secretary added the further comments:

'Capt. William Randall Ponsonby D.S.O. South African Constabulary.

Age on 30th April 1902: 27 years 8 months.

New South Wales mounted police: 2 years

Enlisted Thorneycroft's M.I.   5th November 1899
Lieutenant   "   "   10th December 1899
Captain   "   "   18th December 1900
Captain S. African constabulary   8th April 1901

Mentioned in dispatches 3 times. D.S.O. Medal and six clasps.

War record: Tugela Heights, Relief of Ladysmith, Laing's Nek, Transvaal, Orange River Colony, Cape Colony.

Is a son of Colonel Justinian Gordon Ponsonby (late military attaché, Constantinople)

This officer's original application for a Captain's commission in Cavalry was sent by Maj. Gen. Baden-Powell to this office on 29 September 1901 and was returned to him on 4 October 1901. Lord Kitchener now forwards it for consideration as a special case, the recommendations being very good.'

On the same day, Lord Roberts noted:

'This seems a case for special consideration, a place as Captain in a Cavalry regiment can be found, and he can be sent to a provisional Cavalry regiment on probation. He will be required to join and do duty with a Provisional Cavalry Regiment for one year or longer. If well reported on, his Probationary Commission to be confirmed, and he can then join the regiment to which he is appointed, and assume his proper seniority.'

A letter to the Field Marshal Commanding in Ireland was sent on the 18th August 1902:

'Sir,

I am directed by the Commander in Chief to inform you that Capt. W. R. Ponsonby D.S.O. South African Constabulary has been appointed to the 3rd Dragoon Guards as a Captain on probation.'

Bochym Manor, Cornwall

William's father was living at Bochym Manor in Cornwall; a personal letter from him dated 25th August was attached to the file:

'Colonel Ponsonby presents his compliments to the Military Secretary and would be extremely obliged if he would very kindly inform him whether his son, Captain W. R. Ponsonby, who was gazetted to the 3rd. Dragoon Guards from the South African Constabulary on the 15th inst., thereby be ordered home, and whether on arrival he be granted any specified period of leave of absence.

Colonel Ponsonby begs to be excused for troubling the Military Secretary on such a matter, and only does so as his own immediate plans depend upon the information – which it is of importance to him to have as soon as possible.

Colonel Ponsonby hopes that this occasion might not be considered altogether an unsuitable one for him to express his deep appreciation of this signal mark of approval conferred upon his son by the Commander in Chief.'

I was somewhat mystified by the tone of this letter and wonder if this was simply a mark of respect, or if something more had happened than the papers documented. Was Colonel P. not in touch with his son, or did all communication have to be through official channels? Couldn't he have acquired information directly from William? What exactly was going on here?

A scrawled note dated 29th August from the Adjutant General, said simply

'Captain W. R. Ponsonby ordered home by telegraph with a view to joining 2nd Provisional regiment of dragoons – inform Col. Ponsonby.'

The official documents on file did nothing to suggest what transpired between William and his father when he arrived home on leave. All that could be gleaned from the next few papers and letters was that William never served with the Dragoons. On 27th September 1902, he applied to resign his commission. This was forwarded by his C.O., Lieutenant Colonel De Lisle, and recommended. De Lisle states that 'Captain Ponsonby was not aware that a report had been called for recommending his retention in the service. He has expressed no intention, however, of withdrawing his application to resign.' The note at the end said simply 'Proceed with resignation'.

William married Lilian Patteson Nickalls, the sister of a fellow officer in Thorneycroft's Mounted Infantry, on the 9th November 1902, shortly after resigning his commission. Lilian wrote excitedly of planning their honeymoon in Cannes, "blue skies and gay places after gloomy old England." On the 9th September 1903 their only child, a daughter called Elizabeth Prudence (known as Prue) was born at Fallowfield, Chislehurst, the home of Lilian's parents.
The family moved to the Curragh, Ireland where William served with the Reserve Squad of 3rd Dragoon Guards, and settled at Tore House, Tyrellspass, Westmeath where Lilian took in paying guests, perhaps due to a lack of funds as a result of William's gambling habit. In 1904, a letter from Lillian to her sister-in-law Olive mentions William winning £11 and then £6 at cards. He was late home, but she didn't mind on account of the £11.

Ruins of Torre House 2020

A gap of ten years preceded an application dated 3rd October, 1914, applying for a temporary commission in a cavalry division, for the duration of the war. I noticed William's writing wavered, the date falling off the line. A certificate, also dated 3rd October 1914 stated he was examined by an army medical board, and declared fit for service.

How shocking then, that the next document should be a confidential report dated 11th March 1915 and stating

'Captain W. R. Ponsonby, attached officer, 3rd Dragoon Guards.

This officer is so thoroughly unreliable, slack and incompetent that I could never trust him to act except under direct supervision. His influence over young officers is, I consider, so bad that I hope he may cease to be an "attached officer" and that his connection with the army may be severed.' William had signed, alongside his commanding officer, in a barely legible scrawl.

A report from the medical board, dated 24th March 1915 found him 'unfit for General Service 6 weeks, unfit light duty four weeks. Grant leave 24/3/15 to 21/4/15.'

A neatly penned missive from William, dated 11th April, 1915, from Newtown Hill, Leixlip, Ireland, requested:

'I herewith beg to report myself for orders with a view to being re-examined by a medical board – I also beg to apply that I may be detailed for duty at Cavalry Depot Dublin pending my return to my regiment abroad.'

A note dated 25th April to the Secretary at the War Office in London informs:

'I have the honour to inform you that Capt. W. R. Ponsonby re-joined the 3rd Reserve Cavalry Regiment on 23rd April from expeditionary force.'

However, a letter marked 'Confidential', and dated 8th may 1915, ended William's military career:

'I am directed to inform you that in view of the Confidential Report received from the Expeditionary Force on Temporary Captain W. R. Ponsonby, 3rd reserve regiment of Cavalry, it has been decided to gazette this officer as relinquishing his commission, and the necessary notification will appear in an early Gazette.

I am, therefore, to request that this officer may be so informed.'

William died on the 18th January 1919, at The Grange Cottage, Broadway, Evesham, Worcestershire; the cause of death was Tuberculosis. He was just forty-two years old at the time. The death certificate noted his occupation as Captain 3rd Dragoon Guards, Retired. William's wife Lily was with him at the time.

The Times newspaper obituary report:

'PONSONBY – On the 18th Jan, at The Grange Cottage, Broadway, Capt. William Rundall Ponsonby DSO, late 3rd Dragoon Guards, after a long illness contracted in the service of his country. Age 42.'

William was buried in the cemetery at St Eadburgha, Broadway, Worcestershire. The inscription reads 'In loving memory/of/Captain/William Rundall/Ponsonby D.S.O/3rd Dragoon Guards/Born August 8th 1879/Died January 18th 1919

The Tevis family in America, the UK and Africa

The first recorded event of the Tevis family in America was the marriage of Robert 'the Boatman' to Susanna Davies in Anne Arundel County in 1707, although it is uncertain where the family originated before the American records begin. It may only be coincidence that a marriage took place in 1682 at a church in Halstead, Essex, a stone's throw from where I now live, of Robert Tevis to Honor Smith. In view of the names and dates, and the fact that Honor was a name chosen for one of Robert the Boatman's granddaughters, there is conjecture that the Robert and Honor who married in 1682 were his parents, and of course this is my favourite hypothesis. Robert was imprisoned for unpaid debts in around 1721, and eventually the Maryland General Assembly ordered him to deliver all his worldly goods to his creditors in order have his debts paid and be released from jail. Should he fail in this, the punishment was to be pilloried, and have his ears cut off, from which dire fate he was thankfully spared.

From this inauspicious beginning, the family grew and prospered.

Appendix 2
Lloyd Tevis 20/3/1824 – 24/7/1899

Lloyd Tevis was undoubtedly the 'founding father' of the Tevis fortune, travelling west from Kentucky with the -49ers, as a gold prospector. Luck was not with him regarding this venture, but he soon saw great possibilities in the burgeoning cities of California, and moved to Sacramento accompanied by his older brother, Robert, who had also trained as a lawyer. Robert was killed in 1855, shot through the heart in a duel, after an argument over politics. **(Appendix 11 Tevis & Lippincott duel)**

In Sacramento Lloyd was offered employment in the county recorder's office, where he learned about real estate, and saved part of his salary. Within a few months he was able to buy some land for $250. Within a short while he set up what was to become the famed partnership with an old school friend of Turkish descent – James Ben Ali Haggin. The two men became lifelong partners, and their friendship was cemented by their marrying sisters, both daughters of Colonel Lewis Sanders, also from Kentucky.

During these years Lloyd acquired huge land holdings – the Kern County Land Company, co-owned with James Haggin, possessed a third of a million acres in the San Joaquin Valley, California - and he owned the second largest sheep and cattle holdings in California.

Other business enterprises included the California Steam Navigation Company, California dry dock and California market. Lloyd was also president of Southern Pacific railroad from 1869-1870, president and principal owner of the Pacific Ice Company, and one of the early manufacturers in California of illuminating gas, and joint founder of the Pacific Coast Oil Co, which became Standard oil Company of California and eventually Chevron Corp. In addition, he was a major stockholder in Spring Valley Water Company, Risdon Iron Works and Sutro Tunnel at Virginia City, Nevada. During his long business career Lloyd owned gold and silver mines in California, Utah, Nevada and Idaho, the Anaconda in Montana and the famous Homestake mine in South Dakota, in partnership with James Ben Ali Haggin, and George Hearst. Just two months before his death in 1899, Lloyd received $8 million for the sale of The Anaconda to a syndicate headed by J. D. Rockefeller.

In 1860 Lloyd and James acquired the Rancho del Paso property, where Lloyd lived for a time. In the1880s James Haggin began to breed racehorses at the ranch. There were twenty-four stables with as many as sixty-four stalls in each. A total of 600 horses were at the ranch at one time. Some were famous winners - Waterboy, Africander, Yellow Tail and Irish Lad. James's horse Ben Ali won the Kentucky Derby in 1886.

Meanwhile, the Central Pacific Railroad was being built, which would eventually take over from the Wells Fargo Overland Mail. Lloyd was instrumental in organising Pacific Express to take over the express business on the line, thus weakening the position of Wells Fargo, whose stocks declined from $100 to $13 a dollar a share, at which point Lloyd made a substantial purchase. This led to him being in a position to take over Wells Fargo when his own Pacific Express Company entered into an exclusive ten-year agreement with Central Pacific railroad, for the carrying of mail. The signing of the Treaty of Omaha sealed the deal. Lloyd became president of Wells Fargo on February 8th 1872, a position he held for twenty years, thus becoming the longest serving president in the company's history.

Susan Gano Sanders

Lloyd and his business partner James Haggin married sisters: Susan Gano Sanders and Eliza Jane Sanders, daughters of Colonel Lewis Sanders. Lloyd and Susan married on the 20th April 1854 and were parents of five children; Margaret, Harry Lloyd, Louisa, Hugh and William.

By 1881 Lloyd's active involvement with wide ranging business interests was such, that he was invited by the American Bankers' Association to address their convention held on August 10th at Niagara Falls, on the subject of past and future growth of the industrial and banking system in California. During his address he made reference to the causes of 'boom and bust'; it should come as no surprise that the concern of inflation, fuelled by speculation and unsustainable growth, are the same problems we continue to face today.

Could he have seen into the future, he would have found his words possessed a prophetic quality, 'it is apparent that California's most valuable industries of the future will be that of the vineyard and orchard. California is by nature, the France of America.'

Some insight into Lloyd's character and personality is provided in the Gertrude Bell (1868-1926) letters – written by a lady who was awarded a first-class history degree from Oxford University at a time when very few women obtained a university education. Subsequently Gertrude travelled extensively, recording her experiences in diaries and letters. One such letter, dated 14th February 1898, contains a description of her meeting with Lloyd:

'When we returned to our inn, we found Mr. Tevis and his son (Hugh Tevis Snr.) waiting for us. He is the dearest old man. He came to San Francisco 48 years ago when it was a heap of sand and is full of interesting tales of adventure. He said it was he who advised Lisa's brother to go to the Klondike, that there was no risk, that was how he had laid the foundations of his fortune, and it was the right way to begin.'

The letter continued - 'We made many plans with him and departed at dinner time.........we went to Mr Tevis' house for tea meeting him halfway up. There we found the good Mrs. Tevis and a charming little granddaughter (Alice). We came back just in time to dress and go out to dine at the University Club with Mr Hugh Tevis – the best dinner I have ever eaten and extremely merry. He too seems to have done every sort of thing and lived in every kind of place - he was extremely agreeable. I came away with an enormous bouquet of Californian violets. We all three went to a music hall and came back to our hotel for cold drinks. We parted the best of friends with an invitation to come and stay on the Tevis' Ranch, which we will certainly do some day. On Saturday Maurice took our luggage down to the ship. I went at 11 to see Mr Tevis at his office which is in an enormous building close to the hotel. He took me all over – it is a marvellous place. "This building" he said "is made with as much delicacy and precision as the inside of a watch" – and so it was. We then went out to an immense provision store – built and run by himself – where I bought some tea and was shown all round and given strange fruits to eat. Besides this he owns two ranches, one 500 miles square, a copper mine, a gold mine, iron works, and probably many other things – these were all I happened to hear of. He is a hale and hearty old man, has never had a day's illness and takes all these things in his stride quite as a matter of course. It is a wonderful country. I am quite overcome by the vitality, energy and enterprise of it all. We were dreadfully sorry to leave....'

Lloyd Tevis died on the 24th July 1899 and was buried at Cypress Lawn memorial park, Colma, California. His entire estate, estimated to be worth around $15 million was left to his wife Susan to administer.

Tevis memorial at Cypress Lawn, Colma, California

Appendix 3
Hugh Tevis Snr. 15/12/1860 – 6/6/1901

Hugh, the son of Lloyd and Susan Tevis was born on the 15th December 1860 at San Francisco, California. Hugh had three older siblings; Margaret, Henry Lloyd and Louisa, and in 1863 a fifth child, a son named William Sanders Tevis, completed the family.

Census returns for the year 1870, records Hugh age 9, living in Ward 4, San Francisco with his father Lloyd age 44, occupation Capitalist, mother Susan age 36, brothers and sisters and four servants. The census noted the value of Lloyd's real estate was $500,000 and his personal estate was valued at $1,000,000. In 1872 Hugh's father, Lloyd, became President of Wells Fargo Bank, so it was clearly a very privileged upbringing and from the point of view of material assets the family had everything money could buy. From 1876 to 1880 Hugh attended the prestigious St Pauls School, New Hampshire where he rowed for the Third Halcyon crew.

In 1880 Hugh, age 19, 'at school', once again entered on the census with his family at 1317 Taylor Street, San Francisco.

Hugh Tevis (left) at St Pauls School, New Hampshire

In January 1882 Hugh's 21st birthday was celebrated at the family home. The San Francisco Call reported that a reception was held at the Tevis mansion in honour of their son Hugh's twenty-first birthday:

'An occasion of unusual brilliancy. The ordinary and permanent embellishments of the interior of the house required no elaboration for the special occasion...art has in this private residence one of her temples: beauty written everywhere, with a royal hand; grandeur looking down from the walls where hang paintings from the master's easel.....Flowers rich and rare and fragrant lent their charms to the picture.

The apartments on the main floor are large and numerous.... The parlours, the billiard room and the supper-room, supplemented by the verandas and balconies, afforded an area for promenading, dancing or resting that precluded the discomfort of a jam. At eight o'clock the stream of carriages began to arrive. Mrs. Tevis was assisted in receiving by her daughters – Mrs. Gordon Blanding and Mrs. Breckinridge. Dancing was promptly inaugurated, and continued almost without cessation until three o'clock in the morning.' (The San Francisco Call January 24th, 1882)

The reporter also described the elaborate attire of many of the ladies, showing the time, expense, and effort they put into their gowns:

'Mrs. Tevis was costumed in a robe of royal blue velvet and delicate pink satin-finished silk. The waist and long sweeping train were composed of the velvet, showing at the sides a facing of pink silk. Pink feathers were arranged in her hair. Diamond ornaments.

Mrs. Ben Ali Haggin was attired in a costume of café au lait and a darker shade of silk. The waist, sleeves and sides of skirt were elaborately trimmed with wide passementerie. The back of the skirt was en train, with bouffant drapery, and finished off with a large butterfly bow. Diamond ornaments.'

The California Voters register for 1892 listed Hugh Tevis, Merchant, at 2606 Pacific Avenue, San Francisco, and added the information that he was 5'10 ½, had fair hair and complexion and blue eyes. In 1900 Hugh was head of his own establishment at 1128 Ellis Street, San Francisco. There was a boarder living at the same address, Lansing Kellogg, noted on the census as a Capitalist, as was Hugh. The only other occupant at the time was a Japanese servant.

Hugh was described by the press as a millionaire golfer, footballer, and "all round good fellow", spending his fortune living the high life at various resorts favoured by the rich and famous. In 1890 Hugh married Alice Boalt and they had a daughter, also named Alice. Tragically both Alice's died young, Hugh's wife in 1894, and his daughter in 1901. Hugh was still a relatively young man of forty when he met his second wife, Cornelia Baxter.

Cornelia was the eldest child of George Baxter, one-time territorial governor of Wyoming and cattle king, a self-made millionaire. The family lived on Capitol Hill, Denver, on the Millionaire's row called Grant Street, in a colonial style mansion, where, after completing her schooling at Sacred Heart Finishing School in Paris, Cornelia made her debut as the undisputed queen of Denver society. For a decade the society pages were crammed with stories about her and her many tumultuous love affairs, yet it seems she remained an enigmatic and elusive figure, simply fulfilling the role her father expected of her.

Her affair with Gerald Hughes, a close neighbour of the family on Capitol Hill, was expected to result in their engagement being announced in early 1901. Cornelia spent some time in January of that year at Monterey convalescing from an illness. Gerald joined her for a few days, unaware that Hugh Tevis was also spending time at the Del Monte resort, where his family were frequent visitors. The outcome was that Cornelia broke off her arrangement with Gerald Hughes, and announced instead her impending wedding to Hugh Tevis in April. The couple were married at the Palace Hotel on the 10th April 1901, the bride adorned in white silk, walked to her bridegroom's side surrounded by swathes of Easter lilies, orange blossom and roses.

Who could have guessed that just two months later Hugh would die in Japan while on a honeymoon cruise around the world? Hugh's mother, Susan Gano Tevis left Del Monte as soon as she received the news, in the company of her son Dr Harry Tevis, and grandson Lloyd Tevis Breckenridge, by special train to San Francisco. They had no plans as so little news had so far reached them from Yokohama, except to meet up with Hugh's young daughter Alice there.

'Mourning at Monterey. June 7.—The city board of trustees, on receipt of the news of the death of Hugh Tevis at Yokohama, passed resolutions expressing grief and condolence. Flags were displayed at half-mast.'

Hugh Tevis Junior was born nine months later on the 4/2/1903 at 'Casa de Los Olas' (House of the Waves, pictured left), in Monterey, California, the house that Hugh Senior had built for his bride and never lived in. In 1904 the house was sold to Jack Murray, eventually to be used as a sardine cannery and demolished after WW2.

Appendix 4 Cornelia McGhee Baxter 18/8/1881 – 8/3/1952

Cornelia about 1884

Cornelia was born 18th August 1881 in Knoxville Tennessee, the daughter of George White Baxter and Margaret McGhee. George Baxter was a wealthy cattle rancher near Cheyenne, and one-time Governor of Wyoming whose ancestors came to America from Ireland. By the time of the 1900 US census the family - George, Margaret and their five children were living at Grant Avenue, in the Capitol Hill area of Denver. George's occupation at the time, described as 'President of Western Union Beef Co'.

The book 'Colorado Profiles' conjures a vivid picture of the Baxter family in Denver - 'on Sunday afternoons at the turn of the century, when the weather grew warm and newly mown grass flowed across the broad flanks of Capitol Hill, the powerful people of Denver appeared, like ghosts from a distant winter, ready for new Seasons of exhibition. In pairs and clusters, they strutted the Hill's broad street, women resplendent in gowns from Paris, men in the finest woollen suits that England could make. In the day's heat, under frilled parasols, in swift carriages guided by black drivers and attended by black coachmen, they rode down Broadway as far as it went, then back, then down again, not so much to see, as to be seen by others. And to be admired. Like Thanksgiving and Easter, the great spring promenade was a major Denver ritual, a kind of tribal rite. George Baxter was a prototype. He made and flaunted a fortune. He achieved high social status with it, and when he died, he expected his children to carry on as he had, vigorously and ostentatiously. At least one – his daughter Cornelia - did. In so doing she created a legacy probably unequalled anywhere in the social history of Colorado.' The darling of the Rocky Mountain News, her love affairs, scandals, as well as her clothes and the parties she attended were reported on in great detail, frequently making front page news.

Our story begins as Cornelia returned home from finishing school at the Sacred Heart in Paris, in the company of Gerald Hughes, to whom she had become engaged. The Baxter and Hughes families were close neighbours on Capitol Hill, and the couple had been playmates as children. Cornelia and Gerald Hughes were linked in the society column of the Colorado Mountain Echo, as early as August 20, 1898, when they spent the weekend at Dome Rock, Colorado Springs. The party included Gerald's sister Ethel Hughes, and Genevieve Cooper (later to marry Lawrence C. Phipps). Cornelia and Genevieve were destined to become love rivals for the same man, of which more later.

In December 1900, age eighteen, Cornelia was crowned 'Queen of the Slaves of the Silver Serpent' at a grand ball, the highlight of the season held annually in the capital building of the state of Colorado. Her lavish dress 'of heavy cream satin in the empire style covered with silver embroidery and rare point applique flouncing and adorned with a four-yard train of cream panne velvet lined with pink satin. Around her neck was fastened a seven stranded pearl collar with a diamond clasp and pendant.' One of her maids of honour at the ball was Gerald's sister, Miss Ethel Hughes.

Cornelia and Gerald's wedding was to take place not long after this event, on the 23rd April 1901. Invitations were ordered from Tiffany's, the bridesmaids, best man and ushers selected, and the wedding trousseau complete. However, in January 1901, Cornelia became unwell. To aid recovery, she journeyed with her mother to Monterey on the coast of California to convalesce at the Del Monte hotel, a luxurious resort frequented by the Tevis family. There Cornelia met Hugh Tevis, a widower with a young daughter. Anecdotal evidence suggests that Hugh's daughter Alice (from his first marriage to Alice Boalt), urged her father to meet Cornelia, saying "you have to meet her, daddy, she looks like a princess!". Within a very short while the couple announced their engagement, causing a rift and long-lasting feud with the Hughes family. We will never know if Cornelia's parents were unhappy with her earlier engagement, or previously entertained the idea of a match with Hugh Tevis, described in the press as 'the man above all others who has been the object of all the best laid schemes of matchmaking mamas in California', with an 'exalted social position and Monterey Palace'. Hugh had acquired the property known as 'Casa de las Olas' (House of the Waves) which stretched for over a thousand feet along the waterfront, and was in the process of installing an electric light plant, bowling alley, conservatories and a pier for his yacht. A hundred gardeners were employed to plant and maintain the gardens.

Certainly, it would appear to have been too much to resist, as Cornelia summarily dismissed Gerald Hughes with just a note, or as some reports maintained, a telegram. The newspapers of the time suggest that society was aghast at what had happened; that Gerald had been jilted with so little concern. The Denver Post reported that Hugh courted Cornelia assiduously over a period of several weeks, and they were seen together every day either on the Del Monte golf links, or driving in the Tevis's trap, always in the company of a chaperone. Then they took a drive together with Hugh holding the reigns and no coachman, returning with a ruby and diamond ring on Cornelia's finger.

Gossips also reported that Hugh had been about to marry a young lady by the name of Miss Livingstone, of St Paul, Oakland, although the rumours were vigorously denied. Hugh and Cornelia's courtship had lasted just three weeks, when the San Francisco Examiner of Wednesday 27th March 1901 exclaimed 'Hugh Tevis is to Marry a World-Famous beauty'. The story and photographs covered three pages under the headings of 'Engagement not a surprise', 'The Groom is of noted Family' and 'Case of Love at First Sight'.

Not everyone reported favourably, however, the Aspen Daily Times noting three days after the wedding 'Miss Cornelia Baxter, the girl with the lovely (bank) figure , has married a millionaire at last. Gold always seems to throw a halo of beauty around a girl in Denver and her turned up nose and awkward lines. Money covers more sins and shortcomings than charity.' Cornelia would eventually change her name to Constance, perhaps as an antidote to her frequent changes of heart.

Meanwhile, Cornelia and her mother were busy shopping for the trousseau in San Francisco, where the wedding was to take place. 'While Miss Baxter's wedding gown and summer clothes will all be bought in San Francisco, she has trunks full of other things just fresh from the modistes and milliners and shops of Paris. There are hats by threes and sixes, and evening gowns as only the Parisienne can make them. There is lingerie like mists of the sea, there are gloves, handkerchiefs, chiffon wraps................'

The decision had been made by this time, to keep the wedding as quiet as possible; a return to Denver would have been untenable; the Hughes family, deeply hurt and angered by the slight afforded them, were intent on making life as difficult as possible for the Baxter's. Cornelia seemed unperturbed by the humiliation she had caused, however, making a virtue out of necessity she commented ' Will I be married soon? Now, I haven't set the date and I am not going to tell. Wouldn't I just love to skip away and get married quietly and have no one know. We shall be married very quietly as neither Mr Tevis nor I care for a big affair. I shall wear a white gown of course, with a bridal veil, for I think that's a privilege no girl should let go by. But I shall have no bridesmaids nor maids of honour, just the simplest of weddings. Not even my dearest friends in Denver will be here for it.'

According to the San Francisco Examiner 10th April 1901:

'Miss Cornelia Baxter and Hugh Tevis will be married at the Palace Hotel tonight at 8:30 in the evening. Less than 20 invitations have been sent out. Suite 190, the best in the hotel, has been reserved for the ceremony and repast to follow. The Rev. Dr. Foute of Grace Episcopal Church, who for years has been pastor to the Tevis family, will officiate. A florist and several of his assistants will early this morning decorate the suite of rooms. Roses and pinks will predominate in the main parlour where the ceremony is to take place. Those who will witness the nuptials are Mr and Mrs George W. Baxter, the Misses Margaret, Katherine and Eleanor Baxter, Mrs Lloyd Tevis, Mr and Mrs Gordon Blanding, Lloyd Breckenridge, Miss Florence Breckenridge, Carter

Tevis, Mr and Mrs William S Tevis and Dr Harry Tevis. The list of guests includes no one who is not a relative of either family.'

The bride, dressed in white silk, surrounded by Easter lilies, orange blossom and baskets of roses, could not have envisaged in her wildest dreams, the tragedy about to overtake her. Some said it was a bad omen that the wedding cake, damaged in transit from New York, was never cut. A mere eight weeks later, on the 6th June, Hugh Tevis died on arrival at Yokohama. The cause of death is uncertain; some sources say it was the result of an operation for appendicitis, in those times a dangerous procedure, and other reports named heart failure as the reason. The report from the Los Angeles Herald dated 8th June 1901:

'DEATH FINISHES HUGH TEVIS' WEDDING TRIP Young Widow, Formerly Miss Cornelia Baxter of Denver, Cables the News to Her Father. Former Governor Baxter of Wyoming received a cablegram today from his daughter, Mrs. Hugh Tevis, who is at Yokohama, announcing that her husband was dead and that she would sail for San Francisco at once with the body. The cablegram gave no further particulars. Miss Cornelia Baxter, who was a noted beauty and society belle of this city, was married a few weeks ago in California to Mr. Tevis and they sailed for Yokohama on their honeymoon tour. Hugh Tevis was the second son of Lloyd Tevis, and one of the heirs to the vast estate left by that multi-millionaire. He was about 40 years of age and a graduate of Harvard. While at that university he entered in a mile footrace, which he won, but in doing so exerted himself so severely as to affect his heart. The complaint then contracted never left him, and he was subject to attacks of heart trouble. It is believed by his friends here that a recurrence of this ailment caused his death. Mr. Tevis was twice-married, his first wife being a daughter of Judge Boalt, a prominent jurist of this city. By her he had a daughter, now about 9 years old, who survives him. The first Mrs. Tevis died several years ago, and quite recently Mr. Tevis was married to the daughter of former Governor Baxter of Denver. Their meeting was romantic, and the wedding caused quite a stir in society circles, both here and in Colorado. Mr. Tevis presented to his bride as a wedding gift the deeds to his splendid country home on the cliffs overlooking the sea at Monterey. This place, one of the finest on the coast, is now enlarged and partially rebuilt. It was to have been occupied by Mr. and Mrs. Tevis on their return from their wedding tour, which began at this city and has now been so sadly terminated in the orient. Mr. Tevis was a man of athletic build. a member of many leading clubs and popular among his associates. The news was a distinct shock at the Baxter home. Mr. Tevis started with his bride for a tour of the world, two days after their marriage, which took place at San Francisco on April 10. Several letters had been received from Mr. and Mrs. Tevis since their departure, none of which gave any hint of illness.'

After Hugh's funeral, Cornelia returned home at once, and took up residence at the mansion Hugh had refurbished at Monterey, known as 'Casa de Las Olas' (House of the Waves). On February 5th 1902 Cornelia and Hugh's son, named Hugh for his father, was born at the Monterey mansion.

On the 29th April 1902, not long after Hugh Jnr's birth, Cornelia's mother-in-law, Susan Tevis, died of Bright's disease at her home in Nob Hill, San Francisco. Among the beneficiaries of her fortune of around $10 million were her grandchildren Alice Boalt Tevis and Hugh Tevis Jnr. Less than a year later, ten-year-old Alice Boalt Tevis, passed away on the 15th January 1903, in San Francisco. The little girl was suffering from acute Bright's disease. Alice's death was the fourth to hit the family in quick succession, beginning with Alice's father, Hugh, on 6th June 1901; Susan Tevis 29th April 1902; Lloyd Tevis Breckenridge death by suicide on 25th July 1902 and now Alice. The San Francisco Call of the 17th January 1903 reported; 'Hidden beneath a pall of beautiful orchids, the remains of Alice Boalt Tevis, the little daughter of the late Hugh Tevis, were laid tenderly to rest yesterday afternoon in the Tevis plot In Cypress Lawn Cemetery. The funeral was held from the Tevis home on Taylor Street. The parlour in which the body reposed during the service was filled with fragrant floral pieces sent by the many friends of the deceased. Bishop Nichols and the Rev. R. C. Foute officiated at the house and read the impressive service for the dead at the Episcopal church. The pallbearers were Monford S. Wilson, Horace Blanchard Chase, Clinton E. Worden, C. A. Small, Lansing Kellogg and Charles S. Wheeler. Considerable speculation has arisen as to the effect the death of Alice Boalt Tevis will have on the disposition of the property left by her father and the late Mrs. Susan Tevis. wife of Lloyd Tevis. In accordance with the will made by Hugh Tevis shortly before his death, almost his entire estate of $4,000,000 will now pass to his widow, Mrs. Cornelia Baxter Tevis. When the late Susan Tevis died, she left a large portion of her estate, estimated at $2,500,000, to her granddaughter Alice Boalt Tevis. Under the laws of California this princely sum will now pass to the little son of the late Hugh Tevis and Mrs. Cornelia Baxter Tevis. This little boy, who will come into an immense fortune when he attains his majority, was never seen by his father, as he was born about eight months after Hugh Tevis' death. Thus, a great portion of the Tevis estate will pass into the possession of Mrs. Cornelia Baxter Tevis and her little child.'

The next few years Cornelia travelled extensively. There was plenty for the gossips to get their teeth into, as her name was connected with some famous and infamous men, and she was involved in a number of scandals. On her first visit to New York, Cornelia was introduced to New York society by her cousin Eila, Countess Festetics. Although Cornelia had few acquaintances in New York beyond her cousins, this was soon to change, according to the San Francisco Call: 'It was not long, however, before she met Richard Peters and at his "Open Sesame", all doors swung inward to receive her.' Richard Peters was a cousin of Mrs. John Jacob Astor and leader of the 400, a group of the most influential families in New York. On the 17th June 1903 the San Francisco Call reported 'Beautiful Mrs Hugh Tevis widow of the California millionaire and formerly Miss Cornelia Baxter of Denver is in town stopping with her cousin Countess Festetics (Eila Haggin), at the home of her father Louis T Haggin, 441 Madison Avenue, New York. Society is interested in the rumour that Mrs. Tevis is here to be married, but her friends are positive in their denials.'

Cornelia's latest beau was Ernest A. Wiltsee, a well-known mining expert. Having spent much

MRS. CORNELIA BAXTER TEVIS.
Widow of Hugh Tevis, the Denver millionaire, and famed for her remarkable beauty and romantic career.

time in one another's company at Del Monte, they soon after went on a tour of Mexico City in Wiltsee's motor car. During the summer of 1903 they journeyed to Bar Harbor, where Cornelia lodged with her sister Margaret at their cottage. Here, an incident occurred which was widely reported. Cornelia's fiancé, Ernest A. Wiltsee, came close to fighting a duel with a young naval officer, Lieutenant John R. Edie, and this led to Lieutenant Edie being Court Martialled, although it would seem, on closer enquiry, that the young man did nothing more than sit on the arm of her chair.

Perhaps to escape the scandal circulating around this torrid affair, Cornelia travelled to Europe where, in May 1904, reports of her serious illness from Typhoid fever were circulating. By 16th August that same year Cornelia was on her way back to America, the morning press reporting: 'THE ADVENTURES OF MRS TEVIS Another Sensational One Added to Her List. EARL OF ROSSLYN FOLLOWS HER TO THIS COUNTRY - Her Numerous Love Affairs - Well Known Here.'

At the beginning of October 1904 Cornelia's name began to be linked with that of another suitor, Andrew Hartupee McKee, the newspaper headlines declaring MRS. TEVIS' LOVE AFFAIRS A. Hart McKee Her Latest Infatuation. RUMOR HAS IT THAT THEY WILL SOON MARRY Some of Her Previous Admirers and How They Were Turned Aside by Her.'

'Another chapter to the love episodes of Mrs. Cornelia Tevis, widow of the late Hugh Tevis, is now being published. Mrs. Tevis' latest infatuation is reported to be with A. Hart McKee, a young broker and clubman of New York. He was divorced in Pennsylvania less than two years ago, and cannot marry until the two-year period required by the laws there has expired. Mrs. Tevis has sailed with him on the Baltic for the old world, and the eastern papers report that it is a sure match, and that their marriage may be expected before long.'

Cornelia and Andrew Hartupee McKee were married on the 12th January 1905, at the Hotel Wilson, Philadelphia. A good deal of scandal appears to have preceded the wedding, as Hart McKee was apparently about to wed Genevieve Chandler Phipps. An encounter took place between Genevieve Phipps and Cornelia in New York when they met unexpectedly in McKee's hotel suite. The newspapers at the time reported that Mrs Phipps was 'much shaken in health' when she learned that she was mistaken in her belief that she was McKee's intended bride. Cornelia's parents were also unaware they were to attend the wedding of their daughter until their arrival at the hotel. Within a few days, the pastor who performed the ceremony, Reverend E. Yates of the First Presbyterian Church, expressed his regret at having presided over the event as he 'had not investigated the couple's history and was new to the area.'

The year after the wedding Cornelia gave birth to a son, named Andrew Hartupee McKee Jnr. on the 4th February, 1906. This happy state of affairs did not last, early in 1906 The Wasp, a weekly satire magazine published in San Francisco, was delighted to notify the world at large:

'I hear clouds have appeared in the horizon of the Hart McKees, and their friends are expecting these two sensational people to have a nice little separation scandal of their own. Hart McKee comes from a town of sensation, Pittsburg, and both he and Cornelia Baxter Tevis McKee had given the world repeated shocks. So, it is hardly probable that they will ever cure themselves of the fireworks habit. It is whispered in society that Dr. Harry Tevis daily in his prayers says: "Thank God, her name is no longer Tevis!" The dashing Mrs. Cornelia Baxter Tevis McKee has not, it seems, broken off quite so entirely with San Francisco as report would have it. Indeed, a local couturiere received rather a surprising proof of her regard for San Francisco and San Francisco's style the other day. Upon opening her mail, she was astounded at beholding an order from the much discussed Denver dame for no less than eighteen frocks, to be sent when completed to her New York address. Figure to yourself the surprise of the maker of robes! And again, think of the tribute to our little Western city and its styles, when a lady, who can order her gowns in any city of America or on the Continent, sends away out here for eighteen costumes. That dress-maker's fame is made, for of course no mortal woman could keep such a secret, and since the order and its fame has gone around town the little dressmaker's trade has doubled and tripled, and she is working night and day to keep up with her customers who have arrived since her discovery by the Widow Tevis, now Mrs. Hart McKee.'

Despite the souring of their relationship, it did not prevent the McKee's upward trajectory in society, the Sacramento Union reporting on September 20th 1907:-

'Mr. and Mrs. Hart McKee of Pittsburg are to be presented to the king and queen of Spain. This Information has been given out at Pittsburg by friends of the couple, and great interest and some hilarity is being manifested here in the McKees' attempt to break down the barriers of the European quality. Thus far they have been eminently successful, and mainly through the efforts of Infanta Eulalia, who has been adding materially to her income since her visit to the United States several years ago by introducing rich Americans to the royalty. Mr. McKee was the defendant in one of the most extraordinary divorce cases ever tried in Pittsburg. The present Mrs. McKee was formerly Mrs. Hugh Tevis and originally Miss Cornelia Baxter, known as the greatest beauty in Denver.'

However, during the summer of 1907, Cornelia was already suing for divorce in Paris. There were sensational aspects to the case, as Hart McKee had paid $30,000 to his first wife to keep the details of their divorce out of the papers at the time, as her accusations included 'cruelty and indignities'. On 6th November 1907 the San Francisco Call reported that Hart McKee was suing Cornelia and her father for alleged defamatory articles in newspapers, copies of which they had sent to his mother:-

'PARIS. Nov. 6. — In connection with the pending suit for divorce brought by Mrs. A. Hart McKee against her husband. Counsel for McKee has brought a damage suit against Mrs. McKee and her father Colonel Baxter, because of alleged defamatory declarations made by them and published in American newspapers. McKee charges that clippings containing the newspaper articles complained of were sent by Colonel Baxter to McKee's mother. The court summoned the elder Mrs. McKee and Colonel Baxter to appear November 12 and give testimony in the case.'

10th December 1907 more evidence from the court case was widely published, headlined 'Letters to Sweetheart Santa in Divorce Suit' and 'Chorus Girls Deem Man Generous Whom Wife calls Stingy' and 'Ask him for Gems'. Apparently, Hart McKee's letters were to be used as proof of the allegations.

From the San Francisco Call, December 9th 1907:- 'A voluminous bundle of letters, some of them addressed to "Dear Santa Claus" and others to "Sweetheart Santa," will play an Important part in the divorce case of Mrs. A. Hart McKee against her wealthy young Philadelphia husband in Paris. Just prior to the time when McKee was named correspondent in the divorce case of Lawrence Phipps in Denver, Col., he was living at a hotel in Long Island. This was subsequent to the divorce of his first wife and immediately before his marriage to Mrs. Hugh Tevis. While Mrs. McKee has accused her husband of being penurious, it is asserted he was so lavish toward his women friends that they dubbed him "Santa Claus." His presents were mostly jewelry and costly gowns, while there were many theater parties, midnight suppers and automobile excursions. A Pittsburg woman, who is now here doing detective work for the present Mrs. McKee, wrote two letters to McKee. and is said to have got possession of much of his correspondence.'

On the 26th March 1908 Hart McKee responded to Cornelia's accusations:-

PARIS. March 25. 'It was A. Hart McKee's day in court today. The most notable introduction by Maître Labori was evidence allowing that Mrs. Cornelia Baxter-Tevis-McKee's desire for a divorce is due to the fact of her having brought the Italian Marquis Gugleimi to her feet. The Marquis has been infatuated with Mrs. McKee since 1904.

While Hart McKee was in New York bargaining for his divorce, he and the then Mrs. Hugh Tevis corresponded through letters and telegrams in a certain code and words. A crowded court room listened breathlessly to the wild, passionate outcries of the violet-eyed widow to her absent lover.

In preparing for her journey to New York Mrs. Tevis ordered from a wig maker in London, two red wigs, also red braids with which she disguised herself and sailed in the steamship

Philadelphia on December 24 1904 under the name of Davies, she and a maid servant occupying the cabin. She remained in the Fifth Avenue Hotel disguised for ten days until the divorce was granted. Then she went to Philadelphia, married McKee and sailed for Paris with her hard-won husband.

The hearing continued early in April, newspapers focusing on Cornelia's hat, which her counsel used to support the argument she could not have been guilty of inappropriate behaviour while wearing such an item :-

'Mrs. McKee's Hat Is Counsel's Clincher. Maitre Barboux Uses Fashionable Headgear as Final Argument to Prove Rectitude.

Mrs. Hart McKee

PARIS, April 8.— In an impassioned speech which lasted four hours today, Maitre Barboux, Mrs. Hart-McKee's counsel in the divorce suit brought against her, was exceedingly plain spoken. His direct treatment of the most delicate subjects amused the listeners, among whom were many fashionable women and men. Counsel vehemently denied the charge that his charming client had been guilty of the slightest indiscretion with young Count Gugleimi at the Varennes chateau, which the McKees leased. "The whole story about Mrs. McKee and the count, being discovered by the husband as they emerged from a grove of trees on the grounds of the chateau, is a fabrication." declared Barboux. Only a Frenchman could have clinched his argument on this point as did Barboux. "It is acknowledged, that my client wore a fashionable and becoming hat." he said, "I leave it to your common sense if the peculiar fashion of ladies' hats at the time this alleged incident occurred was not absolutely unfavorable to impromptu love making." Some of the ladies in court smiled approvingly. . . ,

Maitre Barboux accused Hart McKee of manufacturing and padding bills for little Hugh Tevis and charging them to the Tevis estate. "Thus," said Barboux, "the bill at the Hotel La Perouz for the entire family— Hart McKee, his wife, two children and two maids, was $900. Hart McKee charged up to the Tevis estate $615 as little Hugh's share of the expenses. As another instance, Hart McKee bought a carpet for Hugh's dressing room, paying $162 for it. He made out a bill against the Tevis estate for $300." Regarding the earl of Roslyn letters Barboux accused McKee of deliberately trying to deceive the court, as Cornelia herself had shown the letters to Hart McKee before her marriage to him.

Hart McKee's counsel, Maître Labori, replied the following day, as reported in the San Francisco Call 16th April 1908; 'LABORI DECLARES LETTER IS STOLEN' PARIS, April 15— Maitre Labori, counsel for Hart McKee, caused a sensation in his final pleading to the court today by declaring "that a certain letter was stolen from his client March 28th. This letter passed between Marquis Gugleimi, of the Italian embassy here, and Mrs. McKee." Gugleimi is the Italian nobleman whom McKee alleges he saw coming out of a grove, on the grounds of the Varennes chateau one night with Mrs McKee. Maitre Labori accused Anna Barreau, a nursemaid of Mrs McKee's children, of having taken the letter. More important was Labori's proof that the overcharged bills made out for little Hugh on the Tevis estate were drawn up by Mrs. McKee. Hart only copied them at her request.

Labori's answer to the charge of Maitre Barboux that the code dispatches and love letters written from Monte Carlo were partly forged by McKee was dramatic. He laid the pale, perfumed sheets of paper stamped with Cornelia's crest and written over in her dashing handwriting on the Judge's desk with the exclamation : "Once more I prove the peril of written words." For a long time, the Judges and the lawyers pored over these sheets, while Labori read their interpretation in a low voice, so that the women in the court might not hear them. Labori added: "I ask you now, what you think of that charge that Hart read indecent books to her, the woman who could write such letters?"

Ex-Governor Baxter, Cornelia's father, fared ill, Labori showing how he had attempted to get evidence against Hart by writing letters to prominent members of Pittsburg society asking them to assist him to unmask Hart McKee, whom he called "a degenerate of the worst type America has yet produced". Maitre Labori concluded his argument with a severe arraignment of Mrs. McKee, describing her as constantly quarrelling with members of her family and deceiving everybody.'

At the summing up, the general advocate denounced the awful state of immorality brought about by the possession of too much money in the hands of the nouveau riche; "These two persons are victims of wealth and idleness. They are spoiled children of the rich, and must be treated as unfortunate hot house plants grown in an unhappy atmosphere of new wealth." After so much publicity and scandal, the divorce was finally granted 7th May 1908, holding both parties equally responsible as they each accused the other of 'brutal and immoral conduct.' It must have been a relief to all concerned.

It would seem that Cornelia did not in any way alter her behaviour after the divorce from McKee; in November 1909, the ironically titled News Free Press of Lafayette Boulder County, carried an article titled 'THE DREADFUL EMBARRASSMENT OF TOO MANY WOOERS'

'NEW YORK. Pity the sorrows of poor Mrs. Hart McKee , who is rich and beautiful. Those of us who are homely and impecunious are not called upon to face her trials and tribulations—we are not pestered with hordes of suitors. Love notes bring no terrors; an ardent wooer might even vary the monotony of things . But not so for Mrs. McKee; any epistle couched in amatory terms is a jest, a man who says anything more than "the carriage awaits" or "what can we show madame to-day?" is taboo. If men would only stop proposing how happy she would be! But men won't. So, this lady—young, handsome, unattached, dowered with millions—has taken matters into her own hands, says a writer in the New York World. Mrs McKee has called upon a committee of gentlemen to protect her from over-ardent suitors, whose eyes are just as taken with her dollars as her good looks. It would be almost pathetic were it not so amusing. Imagine the situation if you can. This very smart, chic, rich young American matron is actually forced to guard herself from unwelcome attention; to shut the door daily to men of title and position who fall head over heels in love with her—to say nothing of her wealth. Instead of trying to escape her suitors by fleeing from Europe she has called upon her American friends to come there to her rescue. They have formed themselves into a vigilance committee to protect her—and her fortune. Those who read the newspapers must be familiar with the romance that seems to cling close to the life of the beautiful Cornelia Baxter that was. It is a story of Denver, San Francisco, New York, Pittsburg, Paris. Everybody remembers how the beautiful Miss Baxter jilted rich Gerald Hughes of Denver to marry richer Hugh Tevis of San Francisco. Mr Tevis died in Japan on their honeymoon , leaving everything to his beautiful wife.

Mrs . Tevis went first to New York, and then to London . There she met Earl Rosslyn, who became smitten with her beauty—to say nothing of her dollars. The actor-earl was very fascinating and of good family and all that sort of thing, but when Mrs. Tevis heard that his family thought more of her $50,000 a year than they did of her, a brief cable message went under the water. It read: 'Engagement off'. The earl, who had been revelling in congratulations at his great match, was naturally very peevish.

Meanwhile there was a great to-do in the courts of Pittsburg. Hart McKee and his wife, Miss Lydia Sutton that was, were airing their matrimonial infelicities. Mr. McKee settled $ 300,000 upon Mrs. McKee and she got the divorce and the custody of the children. This settled, Mr. McKee was free and he promptly married the young widow of Hugh Tevis, when all the time folks had been linking his name with that of Mrs. Lawrence E. Phipps of Denver, whose domestic troubles were also in the courts. Everybody thought that the beautiful Mrs. Tevis was happily and safely married at last, but—not so fast. They quarrelled. Mr McKee thought that Mrs. McKee was still receiving other suitors and went so far as to say so in court.

Mrs. McKee came back with charges of cruelty and demanded the custody of her two sons, Hugh Tevis and Andre McKee. She even declared that her husband had spent her money and had forced her to live on pickles and sardines. Well, the case came to court. The French judge, with Gallic impartiality, dismissed all Mrs. McKee's 26 charges against her husband and then denounced him for using her letters in court. These French people, exclaimed Mrs. Tevis-McKee, can't seem to understand an honest American woman wanting to get rid of a brutal husband to live quietly with her children. For a year, things went smoothly, and the suitors were easily stood off. Then came Count Apponyi, son of Count Apponyi, the elder, attaché of the Austro-Hungarian legation at Brussels. Mrs. McKee's error. The young Magyar was all attention. He was good looking, of unimpeachable social standing and charming manners. They became engaged. Mrs. Tevis-McKee wrote him many letters, as often fiancées write to the idols of their hearts. In them she called her count her 'cher chou chou' and her 'petit lapin' and her 'pauvre petit dada', meaning that he was her dear cabbage and her little rabbit and her poor little silly. When things got this far the counts' creditors thought it was time for a settlement so they mentioned the matter to him. Certainly, said Apponyi. Then he broached the matter to his rich young fiancée, asking for a loan against their marriage. So, it is my money you wanted after all, cried Mrs. McKee, or words to that effect, and Apponyi got his permission to depart. But he still held the high trump. If he was to be dismissed, then he would show those little love letters to a laughing world. What was a poor, rich, beautiful young woman to do? She cabled to her father, Col G. M. Baxter of Louisville , Kentucky to come right away to Paris. Meanwhile she called upon a trio of friends to act as a committee to protect her, and Messrs. John M. Rusk of Texas, Joshua Brown of Tennessee and William H. Wheeler of New York said they would. And here the matter stands now. The persistent Apponyi is held at arm's length by these husky Americans from being Mrs. McKee's third husband, willy-nilly. It's very hard—this being beautiful, and rich! It has just about got so in this country that as soon as a man gets used to the way his wife looks, she buys a new hat.'

If it might be assumed that Cornelia's reputation would suffer as a result of the divorce; it seems that the opposite occurred. The San Francisco Call dated 11th September 1910 remarked 'From Paris has come word of the marked social success of Mrs. Cornelia Baxter Tevis, who has been voted one of the most beautiful women in the great French capital, noted for its many beautiful women. Mrs. Tevis has been taken up enthusiastically by both the Parisians themselves and by the American colony, her present social position, which is an enviable one dating from the securing of her divorce from her husband, Hart McKee. Because of the attitude he took at the time, and the defamatory things he said against her, Mrs. Tevis social career was made. Her looks, her carriage and her stunning gowns are the talk of Paris and she is invited everywhere.' The San Francisco Call reported excitedly on the 30th October of the same year that 'MRS. BAXTER-TEVIS ENTERS ROYAL SET' and continued 'Leader of Paris Society, Frenchman of Title and Hungarian Count among her admirers. The American colony has been much occupied this fall in speculating upon what will be the next chapter, in the remarkably eventful career of

Mrs. Cornelia Baxter-Tevis. Since her divorce from A. Hart McKee, she is obliged under the French law to drop his name, so she has resumed the name of her first husband, who left her a widow in California with a fortune estimated in millions. Mrs. Tevis' upward march in French society has been so rapid as to be spectacular but this fall, she has added to her victories by entering the exclusive diplomatic set through the aid of royalty in the person of Infanta Eulalia, who was a good friend of Mr. and Mrs. Hart McKee before they were divorced. The Infanta was the guest of honour at a dinner at Mrs. Tevis' artistic home in the Latin quarter when the others present included one ambassador, one minister and several other members of the diplomatic corps.

At another brilliant entertainment this week Mrs. Tevis was one of the most admired guests. This was an exclusive ball given last Sunday night by the duke and duchess de Gramont in their Chateau de Valliere near Paris. Many leaders of Paris society went there in automobiles to dance. There was a play and a Salome dance by countess de Segonzac and Mlle. de St. Saveur. Although this was a gathering of some of the most beautiful women in Paris, many considered that Mrs. Tevis and her sister, Miss Baxter, carried off the palm for beauty. Mrs. Tevis was always the centre of attraction. Many Frenchmen of title have paid court to her, but she has shown particular favour to none since a certain Hungarian count besieged her last winter until she had to flee from his ardent wooing. One of Mrs. Tevis' most devoted attendants is Pierre Deschamps, who is one of the leaders in Paris society. Mrs. Tevis has decided to make Paris her future home.'

'PARIS, Dec. 10th 1910:— Numerous entertainments have been provided by the American colony this week in honour of Grand Duke Boris, a cousin of the czar of Russia, who was dazzled by the bevies of jewel laden American women. One was an elaborate dinner given by Countess Nostetz, the American wife of the military attaché to the Russian embassy. Many Americans were there. Mrs. Cornelia Baxter Tevis, who was divorced recently from Hart McKee was particularly remarked on account of her splendid jewels.'

The divorce did not finally sever ties between Cornelia and the McKee's. The Los Angeles Herald reported on the 8th October 1911 that a new court case was to be tried in Paris, when the McKees would fight for control of their grandson, Andre Hart McKee. They would allege that Cornelia was not fit to bring up the child, and intended to use the revelation that she was now involved in a scandal concerning Nedjib Pasha, the Turkish secretary of state under Sultan Abdul Hamid:- 'Mrs. H. Sellers McKee mother of A. Hart McKee, has brought suit for the custody of her grandson, Baby McKee, thus threatening to reopen the whole divorce case of her son and Mrs. Cornelia Baxter-Tevis-McKee. The child was permitted to spend two days every week with his grandmother. The remainder of the time he is in the custody of his mother. The French courts are loath to separate mother and child unless it is shown that the mother is absolutely unfit to have the custody of the infant. Mrs. H. Sellers McKee, wife of the Pittsburg millionaire and prominent in society, charity and

MRS. CORNELIA BAXTER TEVIS-McKEE AND HER TWO CHILDREN

church work, has made the plea that the child cannot be brought up properly in its environment. Her allegations are likely to open some new chapters and introduce new characters into the domestic drama of the beautiful Mrs. McKee.

Among the names that will be brought in is that of Count Apponyi, secretary of the Austrian embassy at Brussels, prominent among the nobility of Hungary and well known in Paris. He Is a former fiancé of Mrs. Baxter Tevis McKee. It is said she discovered he had no money and broke the engagement. Hadje Hamid Pasha will be another. It was he who assisted Mrs. McKee when she was seeking a divorce. She loaned him stocks and securities and he refused to return them when asked to. But after a threatened suit the securities were returned. The third ardent gallant eager to marry Mrs. Tevis McKee is Prince Jean Ghika. He is a brother of the Prince Ghika who married the Parisian beauty Liane de Pougy and his cousin is pretender to the throne of Albania. The suit of Mrs. H. Sellers McKee is set for trial before the first tribunal of the Seine on Wednesday and her efforts to obtain possession of her grandson promise to be interesting.' The photograph of Cornelia with her sons Hugh Tevis and Andrew McKee is from the St Louis Post, March 9th, 1913.

On the 5th April 1915 Cornelia married Evelyn Murrough O'Brien Toulmin at St George's chapel, Paris. A report from New York at the time stated 'News has been received in this city of the marriage of Mrs. Cornelia Baxter Tevis to Mr Evelyn Toulmin of Paris, France. The bride, a daughter of Mr and Mrs George White Baxter of Knoxville. As Miss Cornelia Baxter she was a beautiful southern belle and since residing in Paris has been prominent in the social life of the American colony. Mr Toulmin is an Englishman and a Director of Lloyds and for several years has been in charge of the Paris branch. The wedding was attended by a large number of friends including the English and American ambassadors. In the absence of Mr Baxter, the American ambassador gave the bride away.'

Evelyn Toulmin was born in 1877 at Hatfield Peverel, Essex, the son of the Reverend Frederick Bransby Toulmin and Katherine O'Brien (sister of the 13th Baron Inchiquin). He was educated at the King's School, Oxford. As a young man he played cricket for both England and Argentina, having lived in Buenos Aires for some years. Cornelia met Evelyn while he was director of Lloyd's, in charge of the Paris branch. The couple had one daughter Katherine Cynthia, born 27th August 1919, Ile De France, Paris. The New York Herald dated 30th August 1919 carried the following announcement: 'A daughter was born on Wednesday to Mr and Mrs Evelyn Toulmin, at their house in Paris, Rue de Saints-Peres. Mr Toulmin is the general manager of Lloyds Bank (France) and the National Provincial Bank (France) Ltd.'

At some point Cornelia changed her first name to Constance, as she appears on the ship's manifest of the Mauretania dated 26th July 1923, as Constance Toulmin.

Constance and Evelyn divorced in Paris in 1931, and it did not take Constance long in finding a new husband. The New York Daily News dated 6th June 1932 informed its readers that 'Mrs. Constance Baxter Toulmin of the Chateau de la Boissiere, Senlis, Paris, from her temporary abode at the Waldorf Astoria, announced last night that she will be married this morning to William M. Gower. She shrouded her surprise decision with much secrecy, refusing to divulge where the ceremony will be held. Both have been married before, Mrs Toulmin to the late Hugh Tevis of San Francisco: Gower to Mrs. Huguette Clark Gower, daughter of the late Senator William A. Clark, copper magnate. Mrs. Toulmin's father was the late Gov. George White Baxter of Tennessee.'

Cornelia, now known as Constance, and her new husband William Gower, returned from honeymoon in October 1932, the Knoxville Journal reported that 'former Knoxvillians Mr and Mrs William McDonald Gower will return from abroad next Saturday. Mr. and Mrs. Gower will occupy a handsome apartment at 1060 Fifth Avenue. Mr and Mrs Gower (the former Mrs. Constance Baxter Toulmin of Paris) were married in Manhattan in June. Mrs. Gower is a conspicuous figure in the American set in Paris, where she formerly occupied the historic mansion on Rue de St. Peres. On their honeymoon Mr. and Mrs. Gower spent the summer in her magnificent Italian villa.'

Constance's daughter Cynthia had her 'coming out' ball in the spring of 1937. The New York Post of February 5th 1937 stated that 'Because of the coronation programme of events the London Season is to be advanced, and debutantes presented earlier than usual. Of special interest to New Yorkers here and in the British capital is the news of the formal coming out party of Miss Cynthia K Toulmin, who is to be introduced on March 16th by her mother Mrs. William Gower, at a large dance at the house leased by her and Mr. Gower at 47 Upper Brook, in London's most fashionable residential district. Last year the Gowers had an apartment at 1 Sutton Place and early summer sailed to Venice where they spent several months at the Palazzo Brandolini on the Grand Canal where Constance Gower's sister and brother-in-law, C. Perry Beadleston often stayed with them.'

In 1938 it was widely reported that Constance's son, Hugh Tevis, sued his mother in the New York Supreme court for the sum of £1,805,397, which he alleged she had diverted from his inheritance and trust funds. Constance denied the claim. 17th March 1938, New York: 'A son against mother law suit involving a family prominent in Bay area society has been filed in the New York Supreme Court. The suit brought by Hugh Tevis, nephew of Will. Tevis Snr. of Burlingame and grandson of Governor George White Baxter to recover funds he alleges his mother diverted from his inheritance and trust funds. The mother, Mrs Constance Leveson-Gower, denied she converted her son's money for her own use. The inheritance comes from Tevis's late father Hugh Tevis of San Francisco and Mrs Susan G Tevis, his grandmother.'

'Leveson' was a new addition to Constance's surname, perhaps referencing the family name of a member of the nobility, the Duke of Sutherland.

On the 17th April 1942 a reporter in New York, Helen Worden, was staying at the same hotel as Constance. Helen wrote for the Knoxville News Sentinel 'A beautiful woman whose name will stir spectacular memories in Knoxville, happened to be staying at my hotel. She is Mrs William MacDonald Gower, better known in Knoxville as the granddaughter of Colonel McGhee, who was president of a southern railway and Governor of Wyoming.

She came from Chevy Chase, Maryland, her present home, to see her fourth husband, Bill Gower, off to England. He left the other day by clipper, on a Red Cross mission. Gower, a big handsome fellow who wears his English clothes with an air, graduated from Princeton in 1925. He has great magnetism and people like him. He did a lot to help organise the British War relief and is said to have quite an important role in the Red Cross mission. There is little in Mrs Gower's voice to show she ever had any connection with the South or West. She speaks with a decided English accent although her mother came from Knoxville and her father was born in North Carolina. The family lived in Denver for a while and it is there that Cornelia left Gerald Hughes waiting at the church. The invitations were out, the gifts sent, the bridesmaids dresses made, when, according to my mother and aunt, who were among those asked to the wedding, Cornelia eloped with Hugh Tevis, a wealthy Californian twice her age. Tevis died in Japan on honeymoon of appendicitis. While he lay dying, he sent for his friend Dr. S. Weir Mitchell, the novelist, who happened to have crossed on the boat with him. He asked Mitchell to have his body cremated and to bring the ashes and his bride back to America. After Cornelia returned to the states, she gave birth to Tevis' child, a boy, whom she named Hugh. In 1904 Cornelia married Hart McKee of Pittsburgh, who had been mentioned in Lawrence Phipps divorce from Genevieve Chandler Phipps. In 1908 Cornelia divorced McKee. She had one son by him – Hart McKee Jnr. In 1915 she married Evelyn Toulmin in Paris. They were divorced. In 1932 she became Mrs. Bill Gower. In 1938 her elder son, Hugh Tevis, sued her and Mr. Toulmin for $1,805,397 which, he claimed, was due him from the estates of his father and grandmother, Mrs Susan Tevis of San Francisco. Cornelia denied the charge and said her son had all that was due to him. At any rate she still has plenty of money, dresses gorgeously and lives well. Not long ago she bought a house in Chevy Chase, Maryland. Every time she comes to New York she haunts the antique shops of

Third Avenue. According to the dealers, she knows what she wants. She also knows quality. She speaks with authority and is inclined to be imperious. Those who are irritated by her dictatorial manner miss the gracious smile with which she punctuates her talk. Whether she has ever been happy is the question. Some think she should have married Gerald Hughes. She might have been happier as his wife but would have missed a lot of fireworks.'

The Knoxville News Sentinel 10th March 1952: 'Mrs Gower Known as Beauty Dies. Mrs Constance Baxter Gower, internationally famous beauty and daughter of the late Mrs George Baxter, the former Miss Margaret McGhee of Knoxville, died in New York City on Saturday. She was 69. Mrs Gower was born in Knoxville while her mother was on a visit to her family here. She was married at 18 to Hugh Tevis of California, who died on their wedding trip in Japan. She later married Andrew Hartupee McKee of Paris, Evelyn Toulmin of England and William Gower of New York. She lived much of her life in Paris. She leaves three children, Hugh Tevis of Rhodesia and South Africa, Andrew McKee of Paris and Countess Cynthia De Lasta of England.

San Francisco Examiner 26th March 1952: 'News of the death of Mrs William Gower, which occurred several weeks ago in New York, will be of interest to all Early Californians. Cornelia was considered one of the most beautiful girls of our country and at an early age was married to Hugh Tevis of California. He died on honeymoon and eventually rumour was put about he had been poisoned, and his body was exhumed, but an autopsy showed he had died of natural causes. Cornelia made a sensationally striking widow in her mourning garb and she will be remembered by many old timers in this dramatic costume, adorned always with a bunch of violets, and seen frequently at the Palace Hotel. She later married Andrew Hartupee McKee of Pittsburg and Evelyn Toulmin, an Englishman, head of Lloyd's Bank, Paris. Residing in their palace of a house in that capital they entertained constantly. At some point Cornelia changed her name to Constance and became one of the great hostesses of the international set of Paris. Her balls, receptions and entertainments made world social news. Of the Toulmin union a daughter was born, now married to Count De Lasta, a Russian, and residing in Montevideo. It was to visit her daughter that Mrs Gower set sail several months before her death. Constance's last marriage was to William Gower, who is younger than Constance's son, Hugh Tevis. In spite of the difference in age, Constance had so retained her youthful looks that the disparity in age could not be surmised. The Gowers continued to reside in Paris and New York where they entertained lavishly. At one time during Constance's years in Paris she had a devoted admirer, a Prince, well known in Europe and the US. It was reported that she would soon be altar bound with her Prince Charming. Then came a robbery. All her priceless jewels were stolen. Later the Prince was accused of the theft and the romance became a thing of the past.

After Constance returned from visiting her daughter she came to New York and remarked to her friends and son, Andre McKee that she had never felt better in her whole life. The next morning, she awoke feeling indisposed. A doctor was summoned who discovered she had extremely high blood pressure. A few hours later she was stricken with a cerebral haemorrhage and died.

Appendix 5
Hugh Tevis Jnr 5/2/1902 – 23/10/1981

Hugh Tevis Jnr never knew his father as the older Hugh died on honeymoon in Japan, from the results of an operation, very perilous at the time, for appendicitis.

Not long after Hugh was born, his mother Cornelia married her second husband Andrew Hartupee McKee, in Paris. A son was born, named Andrew for his father, on the 4/2/1906, four years after his brother Hugh. The marriage was short lived, and after an acrimonious divorce Cornelia went to live with her parents in Denver, Colorado, with both sons. We find Hugh there on the 1910 US census (incorrectly entered as Lloyd), but by 1911, at the age of 9, he appears on the UK census at the Ludgrove School, Wokingham, as a student visitor.

By 1918 Hugh was a pupil at the prestigious College De Normandie located in Cleres, France. The college was modelled on Harrow, pupils learned living languages and there was a great emphasis on sport which was compulsory. The facilities at the school included 5 football fields, a stadium, 7 tennis courts, a basketball court and a weapons room. The curriculum also included crafts, such as carpentry.

MONT-CAUVERT, près CLÈRES (Seine-Inf.) — Collège de Normandie
La Maison des Pommiers

In 1921 Hugh attended Magdalen College, Oxford as a Rhodes scholar which he was granted in recognition of his skill at fencing. The 1922 text of the Magdalen college records:

'Tevis, Hugh; b. Dec. 4 (sic), 1902; s. of the late Hugh Tevis. Educ. College de Normandie ; Commoner of Magdalen since Oct. 1921. Address: 3, Place de l'Opera, Paris.'

The address was probably where his mother was living at the time. Little is known of Hugh's time at Oxford, but Hugh's passport application dated 21/7/1922 indicates he was planning a period of study and travel in France, Germany, Austria, Czecho-Slovakia, Switzerland, Hungary, Italy, and Holland.

Sometime during the mid-1920s he was to meet his first wife, known as 'Prue'.**(Appendix 10 for information on Prue's early life).**

The story handed down is that Hugh Junior met society beauty Elizabeth Prudence Ponsonby on The Mauretania sailing from England to New York in December 1925. On the ship's passenger list Elizabeth was entered as Eliza P. Ponsonby, age 22, Student. Travelling on the same ticket number, 58201, was George A. Evans (aka George Hugh Jocelyn Evans), age 27, novelist, so they were clearly travelling together. The couple also had the same address, 213 Kings Road, Chelsea. However, according to the US immigration record for the Mauretania, dated 14th December 1925, Elizabeth's contact in the US was 'Friend' Mr Geo Tavis (sic), perhaps a disguise for Hugh Tevis, if so, they must have known each other prior to sailing. The story I was told, that Elizabeth (known as Prue) was hoping to escape the confines of a rigorous upbringing by running away to America where she planned to star in silent movies accurate? Or was she already planning to elope with Hugh? The US immigration records Elizabeth's occupation as 'Domestic', suggesting she was also disguising her identity on arrival. (**Appendix 6 for more information on George Evans aka Alan Hillgarth Evans**).

We do know that Elizabeth, billed as Prudence Ponsonby, had appeared in a British silent movie released in June 1924 called Reveille and directed by George Pearson, and there are a number of screen shots of Elizabeth as a young hopeful star. In 1925 she appeared in 'Ragan in Ruins' with Fred Paul. Whatever the reason, Elizabeth did not pursue her acting career. It is assumed that Elizabeth, Hugh and their companions spent some time in New York before moving on to Florida, where Hugh and Elizabeth married at Palm Beach on the 28th January 1926. The witnesses to the marriage were Alan Hillgarth Evans (aka George Hugh Jocelyn Evans), and Alistair Mackintosh **(see appendix 7)**. It is intriguing to speculate the reasons why Elizabeth and Hugh announced their engagement in Palm Beach, but not their marriage. Just days later, on the 4/2/1926 (incidentally Hugh's birthday) an application was

made to purchase an ocean front property on the new Mizner development at Palm Beach. The New York evening post of 12th April 1926 reported: 'Word has been received from London that Mr. Hugh Tevis of California and Miss Elizabeth Prudence Ponsonby of London were married secretly at the Town Hall, Palm Beach on January 18th. A second religious ceremony will be celebrated at St Peter's Eaton Square London, today. Announcement of the secret wedding will be made for the first time at a luncheon to be held after the second ceremony at the Ritz-Carlton Hotel. The marriage was known to only a few close friends including Captain Alistair Mackintosh who was visiting Florida at the time and Mrs Joshua Cosden who recently entertained Miss Ponsonby for a few weeks at her Florida villa Guardiola. The couple will go to Cannes on a wedding trip before returning to London in May. Later they will go to Florida to live.' However, a daily graphic columnist reported that the couple were to make their home at Colonel Fulton's house, near Saxmundham; Cransford Hall.

The Hall, Cransford

On Monday 12th April 1926 Hugh and Elizabeth received the blessing of the church at St Peters, Eaton Square, London. A handwritten card states 'I certify that Hugh Tevis and Elizabeth Prudence Ponsonby, who were married at Palm Beach, U.S.A. on the 28th January 1926 received the Blessing of the Church on Monday April 12th 1926, George H. Colbeck, Precentor.' Elizabeth must have been around four months pregnant by this time; a daughter was born on the 8th September 1926 at Cransford Hall, Suffolk, England (pictured left).

Hugh chose the name Nada from the heroine of a Rider Haggard story, 'Nada the Lily', a name he thought suited her perfectly, because she was so fair.

Hugh's marriage to Prue was brief, culminating in divorce granted January 1929 in Paris, on the grounds of desertion. Exactly why this happened is uncertain. Had Prue discovered the true nature of Hugh's sexuality, or was the marriage a ruse all along, to help Hugh maintain the persona of a heterosexual male and to give Elizabeth her freedom?

When the newlyweds returned to the UK in the summer of 1925 Hugh and his friend Cecil Harcourt-Smith (1899-1956) had a supercharged speedboat, *Bulldog II*, built at Lowestoft, Suffolk. They raced it in the Duke of York's Gold Trophy Races on the Thames in 1925 and 1926, winning the 1925 race. On 11th September 1926, the Bulldog was raced at Lake Windermere Boat Club's regatta along with the Newg. The Bulldog and Newg, both international racing boats, were fitted with open exhausts and super-charged engines, making four times the noise of standard motor boat engines. This upset residents and visitors, who were already grumbling about speed boats on the lake. A report concluded: 'no member shall be allowed to race with a boat having a super-charged engine. The Bulldog, which is owned by Messrs. Harcourt Smith and Hugh Tevis, holds the world's one and half metre hydroplane record. The Newg belongs to Miss Carstairs. ...' [*YP*, Friday, 17 September 1926]

The Rudder, Vol. 43 (1927), p. 51 states that the new Atlantis Gold Challenge Trophy was presented by Hugh Tevis, 'owner of the once famous 1½ litre Bulldog, the first small hydroplane to carry a supercharger.'

Hugh is recorded as purchasing this Rolls Royce Silver Ghost, previously owned by Lord Louis Mountbatten, on the 17th November 1926. The car had been modified by Mountbatten, replacing the car's trademark 'Spirit of Ecstasy' radiator mascot with the figure of a naval signaller, semaphoring the letter 'M' for his own name.

After his divorce, Hugh married Helen Eliza White, nee Woods, in 1934. Born in 1869, Helen was more than thirty years Hugh's senior and was the mother to writer and artist Anna Kavan. The marriage was probably one of convenience for both parties. Anna wrote in unflattering detail of staying with Hugh and her mother in South Africa, where she found herself being introduced as the daughter of *the* Hugh Tevis.

Monterey, his mansion [at Constantia, Cape Town], she described as "a cross between Claridge's and one of the smaller museums" where she had "an amazing gold four-poster bed in which to stay awake at night'. She added: 'Staying with my mother is rather frightful of course . . . this sort of pointless luxury somehow contrives to make itself into a tyrannical machine, so that one is caught up in a perpetual round of drinks, changing one's clothes and so on . . .' [D. A. Callard, *The Case of Anna Kavan: A Biography* (Peter Owen, Ltd, 1992)].

Hugh and Helen were passengers on the Athlone Castle, returning to England from South Africa on the 26th May 1939, and were recorded on the 1939 register (a complete list of everyone in the UK on 29th September) at Claridge's Hotel in West London. On the same page of the register is Hugh's half-brother Andrew McKee, occupation 'Secretary to Hugh Tevis'. For a time, Hugh and Helen lived (perhaps leasing) the manor house at Port Lympne (pictured) shortly before the outbreak of WWII. There is mention of Hugh and Helen opening the gardens of the house to the public. The house was built for Sir Philip Sassoon, and after his death in 1939 was bequeathed to his cousin Hannah Gubbay 'including the cars and planes'

During the 1940's Hugh owned a De Havilland DH 89 aircraft:

DH.89 DRAGON RAPIDE DH.89 fitted with 2x200hp Gipsy Six DH.89A fitted with 2x200hp Gipsy Queen III & small training edge flaps under lower wing. Shipped to S Rhodesia via Cape Town on Sandown Castle 13.12.43; arrived 24.1.44. Damaged beyond repair in hangar collapse in storm Victoria Falls 6.1.55.

In 1942 Hugh was appointed Knight with the Venerable Order of the Hospital of St John of Jerusalem (Knights Hospitallers), and in December 1943 promoted to Commander (Brother), suggesting he was resident in the UK at the time.

Hugh's wife Helen died on the 15th November 1950 in South Africa; Hugh sold the house Monterey, together with most of its contents, in 1952.

It was repurposed as a boy's school, and later a Corporate Headquarters, before being sold once again.

Hugh later married Barbara Jean Stafford Wright, although the date and place of the marriage is not known. Barbara was born 1/4/1917 and baptised on the 19/5/1917 at St Alban, Streatham Park, the daughter of Norman and Olive Wright. On the 1939 register Barbara was recorded living with her parents at Uplands, Reigate, Surrey. Her father was a timber agent, driving for the local stretcher post during the war years, and her mother Mimi worked with the Women's Volunteer Service.

Barbara appears on various ships' passenger lists between 1946 and 1960 with her maiden surname of Wright, so it is assumed Barbara married Hugh sometime after 1960.

On the 11/11/1946 Barbara arrived in New York on the SS Queen Elizabeth, sailing from Southampton and on the 22/2/1947 is recorded on an index card making the border crossing between the US and Canada for the purposes of sightseeing in Buffalo and Niagara Falls. Other information on the card records her occupation as 'Secretary', height 5'10", brown hair and hazel eyes. At the bottom of the card the words 'failed to appear' have been added.

On the 17/12/1953 Barbara sailed, apparently alone, for Singapore on the Willem Ruys.

On the 9/1/1959 Barbara and her parents appear on the passenger list for the SS Kenya bound for Mombasa, Kenya and on the 20/9/1959 Barbara, of no occupation, returned alone from Beira, Mozambique, on the SS Uganda.

The final entry on a ship's passenger list was the 12/6/1960 travelling 1st class on the Uganda; address again entered as Uplands, occupation 'none', country of future permanent residence Southern Rhodesia. Beira was the port at which Barbara was intending to disembark. This may indicate that Barbara was en route to South Africa to marry Hugh, and intended to live there with him. During the 1950s and 60s, before Mozambique gained independence, Beira was a playground for wealthy white Rhodesians.

Barbara loved Hugh, and turned a blind eye to his sexual indiscretions including his long-term relationship with ex-army officer, Tony Shaw, whom I had the pleasure of speaking to on various occasions from his home in Australia. Tony described Hugh as the love of his life, and 'a true gentleman'. Hugh died of heart failure on the 23rd October 1981 at his home, Caesars Grove, Pilgrims Way, Canterbury, Kent. As he lay dying Hugh is reported to have said "Money has been

the ruin of us all" and he should certainly be the one to know, as by the time of his death, the fortune he inherited had dwindled to nothing. Stefan has spoken highly of Barbara's generosity in funding his schooling and looking after him financially after Hugh's money ran out.

Barbara survived another seven years; she died on the 19th December 1988 at Somerton, Frensham Road, Rolfendon Layne, Cranbrook, Kent.

Hugh with his third wife, Barbara Jean Stafford Wright

Appendix 6
Alan Hillgarth Evans (see Oxford Nation biography of Alan Hillgarth by Denis Smyth)

As can be seen in the marriage license below, when Hugh Tevis married Elizabeth Prudence Ponsonby at Palm Beach, Florida on the 28th January 1926, one of the witnesses was Alan Hillgarth Evans:

On the 8th December 1925 Alan Hillgarth Evans, under his original name of George (Hugh Jocelyn) Evans, Novelist, was on board the Mauretania en route to New York. His ticket bore the same number as Elizabeth Prudence Ponsonby's, so it seems they were travelling together. On the passenger manifest Elizabeth is recorded as Eliza P. Ponsonby, Student and the name of her contact in New York – 'Friend Geo. Tavis, Waldorf Hotel'. This seems likely to have been Hugh, although Hugh gave his address in New York as The Knickerbocker Club. George Evans was staying at 'Hotel Chatham.' Hugh and Elizabeth married at the end of January 1926, and their daughter Nada was born nine months later on the 8th September 1926. If Nada was a full-term baby this gives a date of conception of around 22nd – 28th December 1925, Christmas time in fact. It seems very likely, therefore, that Elizabeth and Hugh were already acquainted, perhaps planning marriage, despite the fact that Elizabeth was travelling with George Evans. George must have been a part of their group, which spent some time in New York and then moved on to Palm Beach Florida, where Elizabeth and Hugh's engagement (but not the wedding) was announced in the New York Times on the 29th January. Clearly there was some subterfuge.

A little later in 1926 Hillgarth changed his name from George Hugh Jocelyn Evans to Alan Hugh Hillgarth Evans. He then changed it by deed poll in February 1928 to Alan Hugh Hillgarth. The reason for this remains unclear. Alan Hugh Hillgarth is a fascinating character. It is true he was a novelist and had several books published, but he was also an intelligence officer. After his marriage in 1929 he and his wife lived on the island of Majorca where Hillgarth, a fluent speaker of Spanish, was appointed British vice-consul at Palma in 1932. During WW2 he was controlling MI6 and the Special Operations Executive. He knew Winston Churchill, who thought highly of him, and was a colleague of Ian Fleming.

Appendix 7
Alistair Mackintosh

The second witness to Hugh and Elizabeth's marriage on 28th January 1926 was Ali Mackintosh. Alastair arrived in Miami, Florida just a few days before the wedding, on the Gas Yacht Crimper, sailing from the Bahamas. Just a month later, on the 26th February 1926, Alistair married the actress Constance Talmadge. On the 28/6/1926 the couple were recorded as passengers on the Berengaria, returning to London to stay at the Ritz hotel before a delayed honeymoon touring Scotland. They divorced a little over a year later, in 1927. Newspaper reports at the time confirmed that Constance would not divulge her reasons for the couple splitting up; 'Returns to Film land without British mate and holds her tongue' according to the San Bernardino Sun, 5/10/1926. With friends in theatrical, business and political circles, Alastair epitomised the "Bright Young Things" of the 1920s.

Born in 1889 in Inverness, Scotland, Alastair was educated at Fettes College and after an apprenticeship in engineering at British Aluminium and time at a tea plantation in India, served with the Seaforth Highlanders during WW1. After the war he was on the staff of Lord Leopold Mountbatten and was appointed Equerry to Princess Beatrice, Lord Leopold's mother. He was a popular society figure, and a friend of both the Prince of Wales and the Duke of York, holding a cocktail party for the Windsor's in April 1941 and accompanying them to Nassau later the same year.

He dabbled in many business ventures involving property, night clubs and restaurants, dividing his time between London and Palm Beach, Florida. One magazine described him as Palm Beach's "extra man," escorting all the society women.

He was also a representative and demonstrator for Rolls Royce, and assistant general manager in Europe of United Artists.

Appendix 8
George Bowen De Long

Hugh Tevis's application for a US passport dated 18/6/1918, carried the signature of George B De Long on the identification page, when Hugh returned to the US during WW1.

George stated he had known Hugh for five years; in fact, the two were related as George De Long had married Edith Hunter Lounsberry (nee Haggin) the daughter of James Ben Ali Haggin. James Ben Ali Haggin was Lloyd Tevis's (Hugh' grandfather) brother-in-law and business partner. James and Lloyd married sisters Elizabeth Jane Sanders and Susan Gano Sanders, daughters of Colonel Lewis Sanders of Kentucky.

George De Long was travelling in Albania with his friend Robert Louis Coleman in May 1924 when they were ambushed and murdered. The Oakland Tribune of May 7th described George and Robert as 'merchant tourists' and reported that bandits were to blame. The paper continued 'The murder of Robert Lewis Coleman of San Francisco and George B. Delong of New York, waylaid on the Tirana Soutari high road Sunday, is attributed to highwaymen who infest the back country of this mountainous and sparsely settled European state. Travelers along many of the country roads are an easy prey for these bandits, and the region where the Americans were traveling is amongst the wildest In Albania, a mountainous area where an ambush by highwaymen is easily laid and people on the high roads are constantly exposed to danger. Two men from the American legation here- Messrs. Stephens and Tyler have gone out to the scene of the crime, to make an investigation. They were accompanied by a heavy guard. Martial law has been declared and extended throughout the country so as to prevent any outbreaks that might be caused by the seizure of any person accused of the crime; dealing with an uprising by any of the main tribes which might be ready to take advantage of an act that would weaken the government. The authorities are taking these severe measures and making a rigid investigation, fearing that the crime will have an important repercussion on the country's international status.

63

The names of the murdered Americans were given out by the American embassy as Robert Lewis Coleman of San Francisco and George B. DeLong of New York City. They were on their way to London and New York. A newspaper report dated 17th December 1924 stated that a court martial had decreed that five of the men convicted of the murder were to hang and three others were to serve 10 years imprisonment with hard labour.

Appendix 9

Robert Lewis Coleman 3/7/1870 Yonkers, New York – 6/4/1924 Albania

Robert Coleman may also have been an associate of the Tevis family, as the 1880 US census lists Robert, age 9, resident at 74 Taylor Street, San Francisco. Lloyd Tevis was also resident in Taylor Street at the time. The Coleman's were also a wealthy pioneer family; Robert's father, William Tell Coleman, originally from Kentucky and educated at St. Louis University started a shipping business in California, running a steamship line between San Francisco and New York. He became a president of the 1856 San Francisco Committee of Vigilance, a band of vigilantes set up to combat the lawlessness of the time.

When gold was discovered in California in 1848 it resulted in a huge influx of people (Lloyd Tevis, Hugh's grandfather, was one of them), and among these were many unsavoury characters. This lawless element within the city soon began to bribe, threaten and infiltrate every part of governance; ballots were rigged to such an extent that judges and sheriffs were no longer trusted by the general population.

James King, editor of the San Francisco Bulletin became a champion of the people, constantly challenging the falsehoods and malice in rival newspapers, particularly one run by James Casey, who was also a corrupt politician. This resulted in the two men becoming deadly enemies. Matters came to a head in May 1856, when King exposed Casey as having once been sentenced to a term in the notorious maximum-security New York prison, Sing Sing. Casey waylaid King on his way home, and shot him. King died of his wounds two days later, and this spurred on a group of around 6,000 concerned citizens, merchants and businessmen to form the Committee of Vigilance. As their President, William Tell Coleman determined to clean up the city and rid themselves of the criminals who were taking over. The group was well organised and succeeded in rounding up and hanging three notorious murderers; James P. Casey, Charles Cora and Joseph Hetherington. In addition, around 27 others were required to leave the state, or did so of their own volition.

Appendix 10

Elizabeth Prudence Ponsonby 9th Sep 1903 – 22nd March 1952

Elizabeth, known as Prue, was the daughter of William Rundall Ponsonby and Lilian Patteson

Nickalls. Her parents married on the 9th November 1902 at Chislehurst, Kent. Prue's mother Lilian was the daughter of Sir Patteson Nickalls, a member of the stock exchange

and Liberal candidate for Sevenoaks in 1885. He was president of the Polo and Riding Pony Society. The Patteson Nickalls' were a well-known sporting family; Lilian's brothers, Patteson Womersley Nickalls, Cecil Patteson Nickalls and Morres Nickalls, were leading polo players for Oxford University.

Three teams competed in the 1908 Olympic polo tournament, two English and one Irish, all representing the British Olympic Association. Team Roehampton competitors Charles Miller, George Miller, Patteson Nickalls, and Herbert Wilson of Great Britain won gold.

Guy and Vivian Nickalls, Lilian's cousins, were famous rowers, winning many cups, medals and awards at Henley.

The family lived at Fallowfields, Chislehurst Common, and Prue spent some of her childhood there.

Sometime early in the 1900's Prue moved with her parents to the Curragh, Ireland, where Prue's father William was stationed with the reserve regiment of 3rd Dragoon Guards. Pictures of the time show an idyllic childhood in this remote rural location, although it must have been lonely for an only child.

Prue's mother, Lily, wrote to her sister-in-law Olive that it would be 'rather jolly for Prue having all the children here', in anticipation of a visit from her father-in-law, his second wife, Blanche, and their young family, pictured.

The young boy with the tennis racquet is Bertie Hastings Ponsonby. Described as a cheerful, happy child, he was the eldest son of the colonel's second marriage. Bertie was killed aged only sixteen, in one of the worst accidents to ever befall a ship of the Royal Navy. He was a junior rating on HMS, a fifteen thousand ton warship, one of the navy's finest. On 26th November 1914 she was moored at Kethole Reach on the River Medway, taking on coal from the airship base at Kingsnorth on the Isle of Grain. At 7.50 am, while the crew were having breakfast, a tremendous explosion ripped the ship apart. The explosion could be heard as far away as Southend-on-Sea. A huge cloud of smoke hung over the river, and once that had cleared there was nothing to be seen at the spot where the ship had been moored except an empty expanse of water. In the days that followed the details gradually became clear. Piles of ammunition had been temporarily stacked in gangways deep in the bowels of the ship, and somehow – perhaps from the heat of the nearby boiler room – a shell had exploded, starting the catastrophic blast which killed seven hundred and fifty men.

In 1911 Prudence and her mother Lilian were recorded on the census in the townland of Ballinderry, Westmeath. There is no mention of her father William on the census. By 1919 the family had moved to The Grange Cottage, Broadway, in the Cotswolds, where William died on the 18th January. The move may have been prompted by Willam's failing health; in addition, James Annesley, a fellow officer who served in the same regiment as William, had a home in the village and the two families had friends in common.

The following photographs of Pruee, taken between 1903 and 1918 are from a scrapbook, inscribed 'To Nada, with love from Grannie' (Lilian Patteson Nickalls):

1910   1912

1918

In May 1920 Prue made her debut at the North Cotswold Hunt ball. Her mother was clearly proud of her attractive young daughter, noting 'Prue is very fit and well and has a lovely time and has already a troop of admirers including some of 35! But keeps very sweet and simple'. Soon after this was written Prue caused a scandal when forced to stay overnight with her young man, one Holland-Martin, when their yacht which had left Lymington that morning, could not return due to bad weather. Instead, they landed at Poole where they remained overnight, a very serious matter in those restrictive times.

Appendix 11 The Tevis Lippincott duel

Much has been written, and no doubt altered, in the retelling over the years of the duel between Robert Tevis (Lloyd Tevis's brother), and Dr Charles Lippincott. Accounts vary according to the various political and family allegiances of the story teller, but here are the facts as far as I can ascertain.

Downieville, California, was settled in 1849 during the gold rush, and by the mid 1850's was the largest town in California. It became the county seat when Sierra County was established in 1852.

At the July 4th celebrations in 1855, Robert Tevis, a lawyer at the time, was invited to read the Declaration of Independence. Tevis had political ambitions, a prospective Congressional candidate and member of an extreme pro-slavery faction bitterly opposed to David Broderick, the California Senator and anti-slavery hero. After reading the Declaration, Tevis decided to embark on a long and entirely inappropriate speech, so long in fact, that his audience chose to put an end to his wordiness by firing canons, and making as much noise as they could with cat-calls and general mayhem.

The local newspaper, in fact the only newspaper of the time, was the Sierra Citizen, edited by Dr. Lippincott, who used his two columns in the paper to write a witty and satirical account of the event, mocking Tevis's speech, and his political aspirations, and causing Tevis a great deal of humiliation and upset. Tevis has been described as a 'young hot-headed Southerner with a nervous and excitable disposition and Kentuckian notions of chivalry and honour'. In a state of extreme passion and wounded pride he visited the offices of Calvin McDonald, the proprietor of the newspaper and demanded he print a notice in the paper the following day, calling the author (whom he knew to be Dr Lippincott), a liar, coward and slanderer. Despite McDonald's best efforts to calm the situation, explaining that the article was meant to be taken in a spirit of fun, not as a personal attack, Tevis would not be pacified. If the notice was not published, countered Tevis, then he would hold McDonald accountable. The following day a small corner of the regular news section of the Citizen contained 'The author of the article entitled 'Sad tale of a Know Nothing Youth' in yesterday's Citizen is hereby denounced as a liar and a slanderer' signed Robert Tevis. Although surprised, Dr. Lippincott was not disposed to apologise. The doctor could not ignore the challenge to a duel that this implied. Had he done so, public opinion in California at the time would have ensured he was ostracised from his social circle and considered a coward. The challenge was sent to Tevis, who accepted without delay. Tevis was to choose the weapons, and by a strange quirk of fate, settled on double-barrel shotguns loaded with ounce balls, at thirty paces. Dr. Lippincott was an expert shot with these weapons, having had plenty of practice hunting deer in his home county of Illinois. The duel was fought on the 7th July, at a high plateau amid the mountains, six miles south of Downieville.

Both Tevis and Lippincott travelled on mules; the best animal to convey them over such rugged territory, along with their seconds, and a doctor. Before they could proceed further, the local Sheriff and deputies were seen galloping at breakneck speed towards them. In order to escape their clutches, Tevis and Lippincott crossed the border into the neighbouring jurisdiction where they took up their positions just as dawn was breaking. According to some accounts, Tevis made a serious error, choosing to stand on the higher ground, where he was silhouetted against the sunrise. Described as 'tall, thin and straight as a rail', while Lippincott was 'short, robust, and stocky; both men were 'pale, cool and determined'. Facing each other at thirty paces, the order 'fire' was given and both guns discharged. Robert Tevis was shot through the heart, and died instantly; Lippincott merely lost a lock of his hair. In order to evade the law enforcers who had pursued them, and to escape prosecution, Lippincott escaped to Nevada, where he remained until the furore had died down. At Robert Tevis's funeral huge crowds followed his coffin to the cemetery in Downieville, in an atmosphere of both anger and sorrow.

The incident is said to have haunted Charles Lippincott for the rest of his life. He left California in 1857 for Washington, along with his friend Broderick who was admitted to the US Senate in 1857. Later he moved again to Illinois, where he became Republican State Auditor, and rarely mentioned the affair which had brought about a change in public opinion regarding duelling.

In an ironic twist of fate, David Broderick was killed in a duel in the autumn of 1859. His protagonist was David S. Terry, and the reason for the fight was once again, slavery, the two men holding completely opposite stances on the subject. The duel took place just months before the country descended into civil war and is generally considered to be the last duel of note to have been fought in America.